OCCULT SCIENCE IN INDIA
AND
AMONG THE ANCIENTS

OCCULT SCIENCE IN INDIA
AND
AMONG THE ANCIENTS,

WITH AN ACCOUNT OF THEIR

MYSTIC INITIATIONS, AND THE HISTORY OF SPIRITISM.

BY

LOUIS JACOLLIOT.

TRANSLATED FROM THE FRENCH BY

WILLARD L. FELT.

GYAN

Published by

GYAN

Gyan Publishing House
5, Ansari Road
Daryaganj, New Delhi-110002
Phone: 011-47034999, 9811692060
E-mail: books@gyanbooks.com

Distribution Network
gyanbooks.com
India, USA, Canada, UK, Australia, France

ISBN: 978-81-212-7927-7 (PB)
First Published, 1884

2nd Impression 2023

Printed at: Gyan Press, Delhi.

OCCULT SCIENCE IN INDIA AND AMONG THE ANCIENTS
Author: LOUIS JACOLLIOT, Translator: WILLARD L. FELT

OCCULT SCIENCE IN INDIA

AND

AMONG THE ANCIENTS,

WITH AN ACCOUNT OF THEIR

MYSTIC INITIATIONS, AND THE HISTORY OF SPIRITISM.

BY

LOUIS JACOLLIOT.

Chief Justice of Chandenagur (French East Indies), and of Tahiti (Oceanica)

TRANSLATED FROM THE FRENCH BY

WILLARD L. FELT.

NEW YORK:

THE THEOSOPHICAL PUBLISHING CO.

244 LENOX AVENUE

1908.

PREFACE.

We will lay aside, for the present, our inquiries into the general subject of the primitive civilizations of the far East, and the people who have sprung from the Brahminic stock in the old world, in order to publish the result of such researches as we have been able to make, during our long residence in India, into the subject of occult science, and the practices of those who have been initiated into the sect of the Pitris, which is Sanscrit for spirits or ancestral shades.

This is neither a doctrinal book nor a work of criticism.

We are not called upon to decide, either for or against, the belief in spirits, either *mediating* or *inspiring*, which was held by all who had been initiated in the temples of antiquity, which is to-day the keystone of the philosophical and religious instruction of the Brahmins, and to which many of our Western thinkers and scientists seem inclined to assent.

Being neither an advocate of this belief, nor the opposite, we are, on that account, better able to write its history.

An ardent partisan would have been too credulous, and would have taken everything upon trust. A rabid opponent would have made it his business to disparage and discredit it.

We shall give the words themselves, and set forth things

as they actually were; we shall interpret and explain the *Agrouchada-parikchai*, which is the philosophical compendium of the Hindu spiritists; we shall tell what we saw with our own eyes, and shall faithfully record such explanations as we received from the Brahmins.

We shall pay particular attention to the phenomena which the Fakirs produce at will, which some regard as the manifestations of a superior intervention, and others look upon as the result of a shrewd charlatanism.

Upon this point we have but a word to say.

The facts which are simply magnetic are indisputable, extraordinary as they may seem.

As to the facts which are purely spiritual, we were only able to explain those in which we participated, either as actor or spectator, upon the hypothesis that we were the victims of hallucination—unless we are willing to admit that there was an occult intervention.

We shall describe things just as we saw them, without taking sides in the dispute.

These doctrines were known to the Egyptians, to the Jewish Cabalists, to the people of Finland, to the school of Alexandria, to Philo and his disciples, to the Gauls and to the early Christians, and, as in the case of the Hindus, they set them apart for the use of those who had been initiated. As for the ancient Chaldeans, the practice of popular magic and sorcery seems to have been the utmost limit of their attainments in this direction.

They have also given birth to a peculiar system of moral philosophy, whose place in the general scale of the metaphysical speculations of mankind we shall take occasion to point out.

On the evening before the funeral sraddha is to take place, or on the day itself, he who gives the sraddha should, with all due respect, invite at least three Brahmins, such as those which have been already mentioned.

*
* *

The Brahmin who has been invited to the sraddha of the spirit of the deceased should be entire master of his senses. He should not read the sacred Scriptures, but only recite, in a low tone, the invocations which it is his office to utter, as he should do, likewise, by whom the ceremony is performed.

*
* *

The ancestral spirits, in the invisible state, accompany the Brahmins who have been invited; they go with them, under an aërial form, and occupy a place by their side when they sit down.—(Manu, book iii., slocas 187–188–189.)

*
* *

For a long time previous to their laying aside their mortal envelope, the souls which have practised virtue, like those which inhabit the bodies of Sanyassis and Vanasprathas—*Anchorites and Cenobites—acquire the faculty of conversing with souls that have gone before to the swarga;* that is a sign that the series of their transmigrations upon earth is ended.—(*The words of the ancient Bagavatta, quoted in the Proem of the Agrouchada-Parikchai.*)

FIRST PART.

THE DOCTRINE OF THE PITRIS AND THE OCCULT SCIENCES IN INDIA.

Remember, my son, that there is only one God, the sovereign master and principle of all things, and that the Brahmins should worship Him in secret; but learn also that this is a mystery, which should never be revealed to the vulgar herd:—otherwise great harm may befal you.—(*Words spoken by the Brahmins upon receiving a candidate for initiation according to Vrihaspati.*)

A

CREATION

U

PRESERVATION

M

TRANSFORMATION

OCCULT SCIENCE IN INDIA.

I.

SPIRITISM.

CHAPTER I.

THE INITIATED AT THE ANCIENT TEMPLES.

It is not to the religious writings of antiquity, such as the Vedas, the Zend-Avesta, or the Bible, that we are to look for an accurate expression of the highest thought of the period.

Written to be read, or rather chanted, in the temples, upon great festivals, and framed mainly with a view to priestly domination, these books of the law were not intended to make known to common people the secrets of a science which occupies the leisure moments of the priests and initiated.

"Bear in mind, my son," said the Hindu Brahmin to the neophyte, "that there is but one God, the sovereign master and principle of all things, and that every Brahmin should worship him in secret. Learn also that this is a mystery which should never be revealed to the vulgar herd; otherwise great harm may befal you."

We constantly meet with a similar prohibition in Manu.

The primitive *holy syllable*, composed of the three letters A, U, M, and comprising the Vedic trinity, should be kept secret (Manu, book xi., sloca 265).

These three letters symbolize all the initiatory secrets of the occult sciences.

The *honover*, or primordial germ, is defined in the Zend-Avesta as follows:

"The pure, the holy, the prompt Honover, I tell you plainly, O wise Zoroaster! existed before the sky, before the sea, before the earth, before the animals, before the trees, before fire, son of Ormuzd, before the pure man, before the deous, before the whole world; it existed before there was any substance"—should it not be explained, in its essence, to the magi alone? The common people cannot even know of the existence of this venerated name under penalty of death or madness.

The ancient Cabalists received a similar prohibition in the following passage from the Mishna:

"It is forbidden to explain the history of creation to two persons: or even the history of the *Mercaba*—or, the history of the chariot, treating of the attributes of the unrevealed being—to one alone, unless he is a wise and intelligent man, in which case it is permitted to intrust to him the headings of the chapters."

We are indebted to Mr. A. Frank, of the Institute, the eminent Hebraist, for an explanation of this curious passage of the Jewish Cabala. It will be seen that he confirms the opinion that we have just expressed, that an accurate interpretation of the beliefs of the sacerdotal castes and of the initiated, is not to be found in the works the multitude were allowed to see.

"Evidently this cannot refer to the text of Genesis, or that of Ezekiel, where the prophet describes the vision he saw upon the banks of the Chebar."

"The whole Scriptures, so to speak, were in every body's mouth. From time immemorial, the most scrupulous observers of tradition had deemed it their duty to go through it, at least once a year, in the temple. Moses himself is constantly recommending the study of the law, by which he always means the Pentateuch. Esdras, after the return from the Babylonish captivity, read it aloud before the assembled people. The prohibition, which we have just quoted, cannot possibly refer to the history of the creation or to Ezekiel's vision, which any one might seek to explain himself, or to interpret to others. It refers to an interpretation, or rather to a known, *secretly taught* doctrine—to a science, whose forms, as well as principles, were fixed, since we know how it was divided and that it was separated into chapters, each of which was preceded by a heading. Now, it is to be noted that Ezekiel's vision is totally unlike this; it contains a single chapter and not several—the first one in the works attributed to that prophet."

We see also that this secret doctrine contains two parts, which are not considered equally important, for one could be taught to two persons, while the whole of the other could never be divulged to any one person, even in case of compliance with the severity of the required conditions.

If we are to believe Maïmonides, who was a stranger to the Cabala, though he could not deny its existence, the first half, entitled *The History of the Genesis or Creation*, taught the science of nature. The second, entitled *Mercaba* or the history of the chariot, contained a treatise on theology. This is the accepted opinion of all Cabalists.

Here is another fact which shows the same thing, not less conclusively.

"The Rabbi Jochanan said, one day, to the Rabbi Eliezer: 'Let me teach you the Mercaba.' The latter answered him: 'I am not old enough for that.' When he had grown old, the Rabbi Jochanan died, and after a while the Rabbi Assi came in his turn: 'Let me teach you the Mercaba,' said he; he replied: 'If I had thought myself worthy, I would already have learned it from the Rabbi Jochanan, your master.'"

This shows that, in order to be initiated into the mysterious science of the Mercaba, an eminent position and exalted intellect were not all that were required. The candidate must also have reached a certain age, and even when that condition, which is also observed by modern Cabalists, had been complied with, he did not always feel sure of possessing intellect or moral strength enough to assume the burden of the fearful secrets, which might endanger his religious convictions and the material observances of the law.

Here is a curious example, taken from the Talmud itself, in allegorical terms, of which it afterward gives an explanation.

According to the teachings of the masters, there were four who entered into the garden of delights, and their names are as follows: Ben Asaï, Ben Zoma, Acher, and Rabbi Akiba.

Ben Asaï was over-inquisitive and lost his life. We may apply to him this verse of Scripture: What a precious thing in the eyes of the Lord is the death of his saints.

Ben Zoma also looked, but he lost his reason. His fate justifies the sage's parable: Did you find honey? eat enough to suffice you, for fear that if you take too much your stomach may reject it.

Acher committed ravages among the plants.

Lastly, Akiba entered quietly and came out quietly; for the saint, whose name be blessed, had said: "Spare this old man! he is worthy to serve with glory."

It is hardly possible to construe this passage literally, or to suppose that it refers to a material vision of the splendors of another life, for there is no example in the Talmud of the use of the very mystical language here employed—as applied to paradise. How can we allow, besides, that the contemplation, during life, of the powers who wait upon the elect in heaven, should have caused the loss of life or reason, as in the case of two of the persons mentioned in this legend.

We agree, with the most esteemed authorities of the synagogue, that the *garden of delights*, which the four doctors entered, was merely that mysterious science before spoken of—" terrible for weak intellects, since it often leads to insanity."

We have a reason for giving this long extract in full; apart from the support it lends to our theory, it enables us to show the intimate connection that exists between the doctrines of the ancient Jewish Cabalists and those of the Hindu votaries of the Pitris—or spirits. The latter, indeed, as we shall soon see, only admitted old men to initiation, and their scientific book, the *Agrouchada-parikchai*, as well as the books of the early cabalists—*The Account of the Creation and the Mercaba*, and finally, *The Zohar*—is divided into three parts, treating:

First.—Of the attributes of God.

Second.—Of the world.

Third.—Of the human soul.

In a fourth part, the *Agrouchada-parikchai* sets forth the relations of universal souls to each other, and indicates the modes of evocation by means whereof the Pitris may be induced to manifest themselves to men, and teach them everlasting truth, according to the higher or lower degree of perfection to which they may, individually, have attained through their good works.

The works of the Jewish Cabala, and especially the *Zohar*, do not contain this fourth part. (Not that the Cabalists deny that these disembodied souls can enter into relations with those souls which have not yet laid aside their fleshly envelope.) The evocation of the soul of Samuel, by the witch of Endor in the presence of Saul, as well as of numerous other biblical apparitions, are sufficient to show that the belief existed. But they made it the subject of an initiation, and these terrible secrets were only taught by word of mouth in the mysterious recesses of the temples.

It was not the study of God or the world which drove weak intellects into madness, as mentioned in that passage of the Talmud before spoken of, but rather the cabalistic practice of evocation in the supreme initiation.

"Whoever," says the Talmud, "has learned this secret and keeps it vigilantly, in a pure heart, may reckon upon the love of God and the favor of men; his name inspires respect; his science is in no danger of being forgotten, and he is the heir of two worlds—that we live in, and the world to come."

How can we know the secrets of the world to come, except by communicating with those who live there already.

We shall see that the *Zohar* of the Cabalists, and the *Agrouchada-parikchai* of the Hindus, profess the same ideas as to the primordial germ or God, the world and the soul. We incline, therefore, to the belief that we are correct in thinking that the practises openly taught by the Hindus, were also taught, so to speak, by word of mouth, by the ancient Thanaïms of Judaism.

We find Indian pagodas, indeed, where the fourth part of the Agrouchada is separated from the three others, and forms, so to speak, a book by itself, which would lead to the supposition that it was revealed last and only to a small number of adepts.

We may add that the Cabalists of Judea and the votaries of the Pitris in India, used the same expression to designate the adepts of the occult sciences:

"*He has entered the garden of delights.*"

No doctrinal work upon these matters has come down to us from the Egyptians or the ancient Chaldeans, but the fragmentary inscriptions we do possess show that a higher initiation also existed among both. The great name, the mysterious name, the supreme name, which was known only to *Ea*, was never to be uttered.

Thus, there is no doubt that the initiation in ancient times did not consist of a knowledge of the great religious works of the age, such as the Vedas, the Zend-Avesta, the Bible, etc., which everybody studied, but rather of the admission of a small number of priests and savants to an occult science, which had its genesis, its theology, its philosophy, and its peculiar practices, which it was forbidden to reveal to the vulgar herd.

India has preserved all the manuscript treasures of its primitive civilization. The initiated have never abandoned any of their old beliefs or practices.

It is, therefore, in our power to lift the veil completely from the Brahminic initiations.

After comparing the philosophical doctrines of the adepts of the *Pitris* with those of the Jewish Cabalists, we shall go on to show the relations or connection between the *initiated* of other nations and the *initiated* of the Hindu pagodas.

CHAPTER II.

THE BRAHMINS.

Before touching upon the main point of our subject, it may not be amiss to say a few words about the Brahmins. We do not propose, however, to raise the question of their real origin, which has been the subject of so much scientific controversy. According to some, who have certain ethnological theories of their own to support, they came from the sterile and desolate plains, which extend from the eastern shore of the Caspian Sea to the banks of the Oxus. According to others, who agree with the sacred books and pundits of India upon that point, they originated in the country comprised between the Ganges and the Indus on the one side and the Godavery and the Kristnah on the other. With regard to the former hypothesis we have said elsewhere,[1] "Such a theory seems singular, to say the least, when it is known that this country, which is held out to us as the cradle of the ancient Hindu race, does not possess a ruin, a tradition, a trace, which can furnish an ethnological foundation for such an opinion. This land, which is said to have produced the most astonishing civilization of ancient times, has not a monument or tradition of any sort to show for itself. It would be quite as logical, indeed, to make the Aryans or Brahmins originate in the sandy deserts of Sahara."

* * * * * *

According to the second theory, the Brahmins came

---

[1] The Genesis of Humanity.

originally from the plains of Central Hindustan. This opinion has historic and geographical truth in its favor, as well as the authority of all the learned pundits and of Manu, whose celebrated words are well known:

"Conrouckchetra, Matsya, and the land of Boutchala, which is also called Cauya-Cobja (the Mountain of the Virgin), and Souraswaca, also called Mathoura, form the country adjacent to that of Brahmavarta, *the country of virtuous men*, or, in other words, of the Brahmins."

These countries are included in the quadrilateral formed by the four rivers just named. We shall not dwell upon this point further, however, as it is not our intention to discuss ethnological problems in the present work, but rather to set forth and elucidate religious conceptions.

Manu, the legislator, who sprang from the Temples of India, attributes to the Brahmins a Divine origin.

* * *

For the propagation of the human race, from his *mouth*, from his *arm*, from his *thigh*, from his *foot*, the Sovereign Master produced the Brahmin, priest— the Xchatrya, king—the Vaysia, merchant—the Soudra, slave.

* * *

By his origin, which he derives from the most noble member, because he was the first-born, because he possesses the Holy Scriptures, the Brahmin is, by right, the Lord of all creation.

* * *

Everything that the world contains is the Brahmin's property; by his primogeniture and his eminent birth, he is entitled to everything that exists.

* * *

The Brahmin eats nothing that does not belong to him, receives no garment that is not already his, and bestows no alms from the property of others that does not also belong to him. It is through the Brahmin's generosity that other men enjoy the goods of this world. (Manu, book i.)

This is the original source of the doctrine of divine right.

For several thousand years the Brahmins (priests) ruled over India without dispute. The kings, or, as we might rather say, the chiefs, were only their agents. The mass of the people, like a flock of sheep, maintained the upper classes in luxury and idleness by their labor.

In the temples, which were vast sacerdotal storehouses filled with the treasures accumulated by the toil of the laboring classes, the priests appeared before the eyes of the assembled multitude, clad in gorgeous vestments. Kneeling before idols of wood, granite, or bronze, of their own contrivance, they set an example of the most absurd superstitution. Their principal motive in the performance of their religious duties was the maintenance of their temporal supremacy, and when the sacrifices were over, the Vaysia and Soudra returned to their tasks, the chiefs to their pleasures, and the priests to their mysterious abodes, where they engaged in the study of the sciences and of the highest philosophical and religious speculations.

The hour came when the Xchatrias, or kings, made use of the people to throw off the theocratic yoke, but when they had conquered the priests, and assumed the title of *Lords of Creation*, they abandoned their late allies, and said to the Brahmins:

"Preach to the people the doctrine that we are the elect of God, and we will give you all the wealth and privileges you desire."

That was the basis of their agreement, and for twenty thousand years and more the Soudra, the servum pecus, the people, have never been able to break it up.

Reduced to a purely religious rôle, the Brahmins used

all their power to keep the multitude in ignorance and subserviency. Mistrustful lest some members of their order more ambitious than the rest might, one day or other, seek to further their own ends by stirring up the lower classes to revolt, they placed the secret of their religious belief, of their principles, of their sciences, under the shield of an initiatory ceremony, to the highest grade of which those only were admitted who had completed a novitiate of forty years of passive obedience.

There were three degrees of initiation.

The first included all the Brahmins of the popular cult, or those who officiated at the pagodas, whose business it was to work upon the credulity of the multitude. They were taught to comment upon the three first books of the Vedas, to direct the religious ceremonies, and to perform sacrifices. The Brahmins of the first degree were in constant communication with the people. They were its immediate directors, its *gurus*.

The second degree included the *exorcists*, the *soothsayers*, the *prophets*, and the *evocators of spirits*, whose business it was, in times of difficulty, to act upon the imagination of the masses, through supernatural phenomena. They read and commented upon the Atharva-Veda, which was a collection of magical conjurations.

In the third degree the Brahmins had no direct relations with the populace, the study of all the physical and supernatural forces of the universe being their only occupation. They never appeared outside except through awe-inspiring phenomena, which spectators were not allowed to scrutinize too closely. According to the celebrated Sanscrit sorits, the gods and spirits were at their disposition:

Dêvadinam djagat sarvam.
Mantradinam ta dèvata.
Tan mantram brahmanadinam.
Brahmana mama devata.

Everything that exists is in the power of the gods.
The gods are in the power of magical conjurations.
Magical conjurations are in the power of the Brahmins.
Therefore, the gods are in the power of the Brahmins.

* * *

It was impossible to arrive at the highest degree without having passed through the first two, where a process of weeding, as it were, was constantly going on, having regard to the ability and intelligence of the candidates.

It would have been impossible to conceive of a more effective instrument of social conservatism, and our modern doctrinaires may well regard it with a jealous eye.

Those who were too intelligent, or who were not sufficiently amenable to discipline, owing to their inflexibility of character, were soon lost amid the crowd of bigots and fanatics of the first degree, who were as submissive and free from ambition as could possibly be desired. The lower clergy, if we may be allowed to use the expression, were not much above the level of the rest of the Hindu people, whose superstitions they shared, and whom they taught, perhaps, honestly. Absorbed in the ordinary observances of religious worship, that independence of mind which usually accompanies knowledge was not to be apprehended from them. It was not until twenty years had elapsed that promotion was possible from the first to the second degree, where the veil of the occult sciences first began to be uplifted, and the same period of time was necessary in order to surmount the mysterious barriers of the third degree. That class of initiates studied the *Agrouchada-Parikchai*, or the Book of Spirits.

Above this last degree of initiation was the Supreme Council, under the presidency of the Brahmatma, or supreme chief of all those who had been initiated.

Only a Brahmin who had passed his eightieth year could exercise this pontificate. He was the sole keeper of the elevated formula, which included a summary of all knowledge, and was contained in the three mystic letters—

A

U M

—signifying Creation, Preservation, Transformation. He commented upon them only in the presence of the initiate.

Residing in an immense palace, surrounded by twenty-one walls, the Brahmatma showed himself to the multitude only once a year, encompassed with such pomp and pageantry that his apppearance impressed the imagination of all who saw him, as though they had been in the presence of a God.

The common people thought that he was immortal.

In fact, in order to maintain this belief in the minds of the masses, the death of the Brahmatma and the election of his successor were kept profoundly secret, and were never known by them. Everything occurred in the silence of the temples, and those who had been initiated in the third degree alone took part in his election. Only those who were members of the Supreme Council were eligible.

"Whoever among those who have been initiated into the third degree shall reveal to a profane person a single one of the truths, a single one of the secrets entrusted to his keeping, shall be put to death."[1] The recipient of the revelation met a similar fate.

Finally, to crown the whole system, there existed a higher word than the mysterious monosyllable A, U, M—which made him who possessed the clue to it, almost equal to Brahma himself. The Brahmatma alone possessed it and transmitted it to his successor in a sealed box.

Even now, when the Brahminic authority has sunk so

---

[1] The Sons of God.

low before Mongol and European invasion; when every pagoda has its Brahmatma; this unknown word has been revealed to no human power, and has been kept a profound secret. It was engraved in a golden triangle and carefully kept in a sanctuary of the Temple of Asgartha, of which the Brahmatma alone had the keys. For this reason, also, he wore, upon his tiara, two crossed keys upheld by two kneeling Brahmins, as a sign of the precious deposit which had been entrusted to his care.

This word and triangle were also engraved upon the gem of the ring, which this religious chief wore as a sign of his dignity. It was also set in a golden sun, which stood upon the altar upon which the supreme pontiff offered every morning the sacrifice of the Sarvameda, or sacrifice to all the forces of nature.

At the death of the Brahmatma, his body was burned upon a golden tripod and his ashes secretly thrown into the Ganges. If, in spite of every precaution, a report of his death was bruited abroad, the priests adroitly spread abroad the rumor that the supreme chief had ascended for a time to Swarga (heaven) in the smoke of the sacrifice, but would soon return to the earth.

Numerous revolutions have so thoroughly disturbed the social and religious condition of India, that Brahminism no longer possesses any supreme chief. Each pagoda has its three degrees of initiation, and its own private Brahmatma. The chiefs of these temples are often at open hostility with each other. However, this does not seem to have affected their religious belief, as yet, and we shall see, as we study the methods in use in the three different classes of initiation, that the Hindu Brahmins still cling to their old religious prescriptions.

CHAPTER III.

THE BRAHMIN—FROM HIS BIRTH TO HIS NOVITIATE—THE CEREMONY OF THE DJITA CARMA.

When a Brahmin's wife has given birth to a son, her husband is careful to note upon his tablets the hour, the day, the year, and the epoch, of the occurrence, together with the stars under whose auspices the child has just been born.

He carries this information to the astronomer of the pagoda, who casts the horoscope of the new-born child. Nine days thereafter a stand is erected and decorated with flowers and foliage, upon which the mother takes her seat, with the boy in her arms.

An officiating Pourohita, or Brahmin belonging to the first class of initiation, then performs the poudja, or sacrifice to Vischnou, in front of the stand. He pours a little lustral water upon the child's head, and into the hollow of the hands of the father and mother, who drink it, and then he sprinkles all those present with the same liquid.

The father then brings a dish of earthenware, bronze, or silver, according to his means, upon which is a little betel, and a present for the Pourohita.

By this ceremony the child is purified from all the uncleanness attached to his birth.

From this time, the mother, who since her confinement, has stayed in a separate room, is obliged to live ten days longer by herself in a retired place, at the end of which time she is allowed to go to the temple, to purify herself from her uncleanness.

It is unnecessary to call attention to the fact that a similar custom in such cases prevailed among the Jews.

The Ceremony of the Nahma-Carma.

Twelve days afterward the ceremony of the giving of the name, or of the Nahma-Carma, as it was called, took place.

The house was decorated as if for a festival, and all the relatives and friends of the Brahmin caste alone were invited.

The father, after performing an oblation to the fire and the nine principal divinities which rule the planets, transcribed with a brush upon a wooden tablet the horoscope of his son, which was cast at the pagoda, with the name that he proposed to give him.

He then uttered three times in a loud voice the name which he had just written, which all present repeated after him. He closed with the following words:

"Blessed be the name of Brahma. This is my son and his name is Narayana [or any other name]. Listen attentively in order that you may remember it."

He then went out of the house at the head of a procession consisting of all his guests, and planted in his garden, or in front of the dwelling, a cocoanut, tamarind, or palm tree, according to the section of country where he resided, saying:

"In the name of the powerful and just Brahma, all you who are here present, bear this in mind. This tree is planted on Narayana's name-day, in the thirty-fifth year of the fifth lunar century of the third divine epoch" (or any given date).

This, as the reader will understand, is given merely as a matter of form.

At the close of the ceremony, a grand feast is given, of

which all present partake. Previous to their departure, the father presents to each a cup of cedar- or sandal-wood, upon which is engraved the horoscope, or more generally the monogram of the child.

The object of this present is to furnish evidence, in case any dispute should thereafter arise as to the legitimacy of the child's birth. When summoned as witnesses before the caste tribunal, the guests appear with their cups in their hands, and testify as follows:

"In the name of the powerful and just Brahma; the words which proceed from my mouth are strictly true. This cup was given to me by Covinda, on Narayana's name-day, in the thirty-fifth year of the fifth lunar century of the third divine epoch. There can be no doubt that Narayana is the son of Covinda."

The Pourohita, or Brahmin who is present at the ceremony, then offers a sacrifice to the Pitris, or ancestral spirits, and asks them to protect the new-born child.

The father then distributes betel among the guests and makes a present to the officiating priest according to his means.

The Ceremony of Anna-Prassana.

When the child is in the seventh month of his age, rice is given him to eat for the first time. This festival is called the *Anna-Prassana.*

As in the case of the other ceremonies the father invites all his relatives and friends and sends to the pagoda for a Brahmin to officiate. After a general bath in the tank of ablutions, upon which the Pourohita has scattered a few drops of lustral water, all the guests take their seats upon a stand decorated with branches of fruit-trees in full bearing, and the priest offers a sacrifice to the lunar spirits that protect the family.

Meanwhile, the women sing an appropriate psalm and

perform the ceremony of aratty (which has the property of driving away evil spirits) above the child's head for the first time.

The priest then blesses the Brahminical girdle which is a sign of his caste, and which is bound around the child's loins for the first time. A little boiled rice is then put in his mouth, and everybody sits down to the repast.

The ceremony terminates with the distribution of betel and a present to the officiating priest.

The Ceremony of the Tchaoula.

When a child reaches the age of three years, the ceremony of the Tchaoula, or the Tonsure, is performed.

This festival is much more solemn than the preceding, for the child, who is present, is able for the first time to murmur the name of the divinity, as well as the names of the protecting spirits of his home and family.

After bathing and decorating the child with a necklace and bracelets of mingled coral and sandal-wood beads, he is led beneath a pandal, which is a sort of dais formed of trees procured for that purpose and of flowers of every description.

He is surrounded by his relatives and guests and the priest offers an oblation to all the Pitris, or family and ancestral shades, in both branches, on the father's and mother's side.

The statue of Siva-Lingam, the image of perpetual fruitfulness, is brought in covered with flowers and fruits.

At this point of the office the barber commences. After prostrating himself in the presence of the god, in the midst of female singing, accompanied by the musicians from the pagoda, he proceeds to shave the child's head, leaving a small lock of hair on the back part, which is never cut.

During this operation the child's female relatives perform the aratty upon the heads of those present, in order to drive away evil spirits, and everybody preserves a religious silence.

Having finished his duties, the barber retires with his pay, which consists of a certain quantity of rice, and the priest cleanses the child from any impurity which he may have derived from unclean contact with the barber.

The child's toilet is then made anew, and after a fresh bath in the sacred tank of ablutions, in order to propitiate all the spirits and genii of the plants to which that day is consecrated the ceremony closes as before with a repast and presents.

Until the age of nine years the Brahmin remains in the hands of the women until the term for commencing his novitiate arrives.

CHAPTER IV.

THE BRAHMIN—FROM HIS NOVITIATE TO HIS RECEPTION INTO THE FIRST DEGREE OF HIS INITIATION.

The Ceremony of Oupanayana.

[Taken from the Nitia-Carma, the first part of the Agrouchada-Parikchai, or book of the occult sciences of the Brahmins.]

The word Oupanayana signifies introduction to the study of the sciences. We give this passage of the Agrouchada in the form of verses, as it was written:

It is now time for the virtuous father, who possesses a son over whose head has rolled three times three years, the figure of the tutelary spirits, to perform the ceremony of the Oupanayana.

* * *

He should procure vessels of gold, silver, bronze, or earthenware, according to his means, which are to be distributed to the Brahmins after the repast.

* * *

He should lay in an abundant supply of rice, seeds, fruit, oil, butter, sugar, vegetables, and milk, for he has not only to entertain his guests, but the larger part should be offered as an oblation to the Pitris, or set apart for the poor and orphans.

* * *

When the father of a family gives food to the suffering,

to returning travellers, to pilgrims, and to little children who look in curiously at the feast with envious eyes as they pass, when, like a sower, he scatters outdoors handfuls of seeds for the little birds, the spirits and his ancestral shades are content.

* * *

The festival should last four days, and new vessels and fresh and pure provisions should be used daily.

* * *

He should prepare powdered vermilion, sandal-wood, and saffron, in order that the women may trace magic circles around the house to drive away evil spirits and attract good spirits.

* * *

These preparations being completed, the father should ask the Pourohita to name a day of auspicious omen. It should never be at the commencement nor at the end of the moon. It should never either be an odd day.

* * *

The pandal should then be erected with consecrated flowers and foliage, among which the lotus flower should predominate. He should then spread upon the ground a thick layer of cousa grass, and he should invite his relatives, commencing with those in the ascending line on the father's side, after which he should bid his friends and all Brahmins who have reached the age of one hundred years.

* * *

The women should sumptuously decorate the pandal with hanging garlands and bouquets of flowers so as to form alternate bands of red and white.

* * *

All the guests before going to the place where the ceremony is to be held, should perform the usual purifications in the sacred tank of the pagoda.

***

When the parents and friends are all assembled the Pourohita should be introduced with all due marks of respect. He should bring with him a girdle and the skin of a gazelle. A gazelle's skin is always pure, and he who sits thereon does not contract any uncleanness.

***

The Pourohita should then perform the san-colpa, or preparation of the soul, in which he is absorbed in the contemplation of Vischnou, who is represented as the author and preserver of the universe.

***

He should regard him as a distributor of every favor, and as one who crowns with success all our enterprises. With this view he should pronounce his name three times and offer him adoration.

***

He should then contemplate the infinite perfection of Brahma. He should ponder over the three triads,[1] which have sprung from him, and have created the eight million four hundred thousand kinds of living creatures, at the head of which is man.

***

He should then ponder over the existence of the universe, which is to last a hundred years of the gods,[2] which are divided into four periods, of which the first, second, and half of the third have already elapsed. He should then perform an oblation to the universe.

---

[1] Nara-Nari-Viradj *** Ayni-Voya-Sourya * Brahma * Vischnou-Siva.

[2] Each year of the gods is equal to several thousands of the lunar years.

He should think of the different incarnations of Vischnou, and of that of the boar under whose form the god vanquished the giant Hirannia.

* * *

He should prostrate himself before the fourteen categories of celestial (Pitris) and inferior spirits by which the universe is filled.

* * *

He should perform an oblation to the pure fluid which is called Agasa, and which is the essence of life.

* * *

He should pronounce the mysterious monosyllable which was to be kept from the knowledge of the multitude, by merely moving his lips.

* * *

He should offer sacrifice to Swayambhouva, the self-existent being.

* * *

He should evoke the spirits of his ancestors and ask them to be present at the ceremony.

* * *

He should drive away all evil spirits whose presence might otherwise disturb the sacrifices.

* * *

He should propitiate the superior spirit Poulear, who presides over obstacles and brings enterprises to a successful issue.

* * *

All the guests should repair again to the sacred tank of ablution, where they purify themselves according to their method prescribed.

Upon their return the Brahmatchary, or neophyte, should take his place beneath the pandal of flowers, and all the married women present should chant consecrated psalms and at the same time anoint his limbs with perfumed oil and saffron and rub his eyelids with antimony.

* * *

When his toilet is finished the father and mother of the neophyte should take their place by his side beneath the pandal, and the women should perform upon their heads the ceremony of the aratty, in order to remove evil omens.

* * *

The Poudja, or sacrifice, is then offered to all the tutelary spirits of the family, as well as the firstlings of all the dishes prepared for the repast.

* * *

All the men and women should then sit down on cocoanut leaves covered with lotus leaves, and should turn their backs so that they may not see each other eat.

* * *

Rice, clarified butter, oil, sugar, fruits, and vegetables are then brought in for the feast, and at the close of the repast the father distributes betel and gives a present to the Pourohita, after which everybody retires.

* * *

Such was the first day of the Oupanayana.

* * *

The next day was called Mouhourta, or the great day, for it was that on which the neophyte was to be invested with the girdle.

* * *

The Brahmatchary should take his place beneath the

pandal, between his father and mother, and all three should turn their faces toward the East.

* * *

The Brahmatchary should have his loins girt around with new linen of pure material, and the women should gently rub his chest and arms with the powdered saffron and sandal-wood mingled, and should sing consecrated psalms.

* * *

The Pourohita should then advance with a silver furnace filled with burning coals: he should perform the sacrifice to the spirits, by evoking them around the fire, and should throw incense and powdered sandal-wood upon the fire, to gratify their sense of smell.

* * *

This fire should be carefully kept until the end of the festival Oupanayana, for if it should happen to be extinguished, great harm might ensue, and the familiar spirits might desert the house.

* * *

The preservation of this fire should be given in charge to nine Brahmins and their wives.

* * *

All the married women who happen to be among the guests should go in great pomp to the consecrated tank, preceded by musical instruments, and bearing a copper vessel, which they are to fill with water.

* * *

Upon their return to the house they should cover the mouth of the vessel with mango leaves, and hang above it a branch of a banana tree, freshly cut, with all its fruits.

They should all then go together to the neighboring forest, where, having found a nest of white ants, they should fill ten earthen pots with earth beaten and sifted by these animals.

* * *

Returning then to the other guests, they should plant in these pots ten different kinds of seeds, which they should sprinkle with water taken from the sacred tank.

* * *

When this has been done, the Pourohita should bring all the pots together and stretch over them a fine cloth; he should recite the invocation to the tutelary spirits and ask them to manifest their power by auspicious omens.

* * *

Imposing his hands above the cloth, he should then pronounce in a low voice, unheard by those present, the following magic words:

Agnim-Pâ-Pâtra.
Paryâya.
Parôxa.

These are Sanscrit words, signifying:

Agnim—sacred fire,
Pâ—holy water,
Pâtra—purified vessel,
Paryáya—magic vegetation,
Parôxa—invisible.

The Pourohita should utter these words nine times nine times. The tutelary spirits will then manifest themselves and the cloth is gradually raised during the continuance of the invocation.

* * *

The Pourohita should then remove the cloth, and he will find that the ten seeds have appeared above the earth in the ten pots, and ten shrubs have grown as high as the Pourohita's forehead, bearing flowers and fruits each after its kind.

* * *

The Brahmatchary's mother should then weave a crown of flowers gathered from these trees, and should place it upon her son's head. The Pourohita should then distribute among all of those present the fruits which have grown beneath the cloth, which the guests should eat, repeating the following words three times:

The auspicious omen has manifested itself.
The auspicious omen has manifested itself.
The auspicious omen has manifested itself.

The Brahmatchary then receives the triple cord of the novitiate.

* * *

A new invocation was then made to the spirits of the planets and ancestors, thanking them for their protection and intervention, and a piece of consecrated saffron was attached about the young Brahmin's neck.

* * *

The barber should then shave the neophyte's head and cut the nails of his feet and hands to the sound of the women's songs, accompanied by the musician from the pagoda.

* * *

The young Brahmin is then required to take a bath in the tank of ablution, in order to remove any impurity which he may have contracted by being in contact with the barber, who is unclean, and the women attire him in new and pure linen garments.

* * *

The Pourohita then advances to his side and, by the imposition of hands, removes his ignorance and qualifies him for the study of the sciences, which will now occupy every moment of his time. He should then gird about his waist a triple girdle, woven from the sacred grass of the Darba.

* * *

Reciting the conjurations of the neck and bosom, the Pourohita then decorates the neophyte with the triple girdle of the Brahminic initiation, and consecrates him Brahmatchary or candidate for initiation.

* * *

At this time a Guru, or master of the sacred science, is chosen for the young Brahmatchary. He must be more than sixty years old.

* * *

The Guru should take his new pupil aside, and turning his face toward the East, he should say to him, "Oh! my son, you have now taken your seat by the side of men, may your body be free from all impurity; may your thoughts always turn toward the good, for Brahma will now commence to know you by your actions.

* * *

"Know that the shades of your ancestors in an aërial form will attend you in all your studies, and will reveal to you hereafter, if you are worthy, the grand secret of being.

* * *

"Always bear in mind that what you will now learn should never be revealed to the vulgar herd, and that you will never arrive at the end of your initiation if you are unable to hide the secret of things in the deepest recesses of your heart."

* * *

Having uttered these words, the Guru for the first time calls the young Bramatchary, Douidja, which means twice born.

The first birth is merely the advent into material life, the second birth is the entrance to a spiritual life.

* * *

So ends the second day.

* * *

On the third day the Brahmatchary for the first time offers a sacrifice to fire, and performs an oblation to the spirits and to his ancestral shades, in the presence of all the guests.

* * *

On the fourth day the father of the young Brahmin who has just received the investiture should make suitable presents to all the Brahmins who were present at the ceremony, and should not forget to give a cow and a hundred manganys of rice to his son's Guru.

* * *

Having repeated the san-colpa, the Pourohita should perform an oblation to all the spirits that he evoked to be present at the festival, and he should thank them for answering his summons.

* * *

All present should say as they separate, "The child is dead, a man is born."

* * *

We purposely refrain from accompanying this curious passage from the Agrouchada-Parikchai with any comments of our own. As we have said before, we merely propose to give an impartial account of these strange customs.

We will say, however, that in this ceremony of the Oupanayana or investiture of the sacred girdle, which makes a man of the boy, the Pitris, or spirits, and the ancestral shades take the most prominent part. They are evoked by a Pourohita, they are present during the whole festival, and they almost exclusively receive the sacrifice, oblations, and firstlings of all the dishes prepared for the repast which terminates the mysterious celebrations of each particular day.

Vischnou, as well as Brahma, the lord of all beings, and the master of gods and men, is only evoked by the Pourohita in order to prepare himself for the ceremony by the contemplation of the perfections of the creator and preserver of the universe.

The Brahmatchary continues his studies as novice until the time of his marriage, which takes place about the sixteenth or eighteenth year of his age. During this period he lives with his Guru, or director, and engages in the study of the sacred books, and of the mathematical and astronomical sciences.

He is not yet admitted to the study of the *occult sciences*, whose first principles he will only begin to learn when he has reached the degree of Grihasta, or head of a family, or of Pourohita, or officiating priest.

The following instructions are taken from Manu:

After the initiation of the Brahmatchary, the Guru teaches him the duty of purity and morality, the maintenance of the sacred fire, and the morning, noon, and evening sandyas, which are a kind of prayers.

* * *

After having performed the prescribed ablutions, and before opening the Veda, turning his face toward the East, the Brahmatchary should pay homage to the sovereign master of the universe.

* * *

During the reading of the Veda he should control his senses, and stand with clasped hands in an attitude of homage before the sacred scriptures. At the commencement and close of the reading, he should kiss the feet of his director, and not commence nor stop until he hears the Guru tell him to begin his studies or to desist.

*
* *

Always, at the commencement or end of his reading, he should pronounce the sacred monosyllable, A, U, M, which contains the mystery of the Trinity. That will make him remember what he has learned, otherwise it will vanish like letters traced upon the waters.

*
* *

He should pronounce this mysterious monosyllable, which is an invocation to the Trimourti and which expresses the substance of the Veda, according to Brahma himself, with face turned toward the East; he should be free from all impurity, should hold his breath, and have in his hands a stalk of sacred cousa grass.

*
* *

The Brahmatchary should never cause the slighest trouble to the Guru who has undertaken to educate him and to instruct him in the knowledge of the sacred scriptures. He should venerate him like a father and mother.

It nowhere appears in the Agrouchada-Parikchai that it is lawful for the Brahmatchary to make use of the invocation of the mysterious monosyllable, A, U, M, as he is allowed to do by Manu, but the ancient legislator uses the word here in its vulgar sense, in which it represents the religious triad; as for the mystical signification of the three letters, he forbids its explanation, like the book of the Pitris.

*
* *

The primitive holy syllable, composed of the three letters, in which the vedic trinity is comprised, should be kept secret. (Manu, book xi., sloca 265.)

We shall not describe in the present work the Brahmatchary's marriage ceremony nor his funeral, in case of his death before his novitiate is completed. The restricted limits of a single volume will not allow us to dwell upon these matters except at the expense of the more interesting parts of our subject.

The real practice of the occult sciences did not commence until the second or third degree of initiation. It is mainly important that we should make ourselves acquainted with these, the novitiate and the first class of initiation being only preparatory to the higher degrees.

Suffice it to say that the evocation of the ancestral shades of the Pitris always formed a prominent feature, both of the marriage ceremony and of the funeral rites. They could not take place without their being present.

CHAPTER V.

THE FIRST DEGREE OF INITIATION—ABLUTIONS—PRAYER—CEREMONIES—EVOCATION.

[Taken from the Agrouchada-Parikchai.]

After his marriage, the Brahmatchary left the class of neophytes, but he did not, however, enter that of the Grihastas, or heads of family, who had been admitted to the first degree of initiation. In order to do so, it was requisite, first, that he should have paid his ancestors' debt by the birth of a son, who would perpetuate their race; second, that he should be deemed worthy, upon the report of his Guru, of taking this step.

Upon admission he might remain a simple Grihasta, or he might be attached to the service of a pagoda, in the capacity of a Pourohita; in either case, he was now a member of the great sacerdotal family, and during twenty years all the acts of his daily life would be instrumental in the preparation, both mentally and physically, by meditation, prayers, sacrifices, ablutions, and the strictest attention to personal cleanliness, for the superior transformation which was now the object of all his efforts.

According to the first part of the Agrouchada-Parikchai, which we have already quoted, and which is called the Nittia-Carma, the following is an account of the innumerable corporeal and spiritual purifications which were enjoined upon him, and none of which could be neglected under the severest penalties.

They are divided in the original work in the following manner:

Proemium.

* * *

The Grihasta should leave his mat every morning before sunrise, and his first words, upon leaving his bed, should be an invocation to Vischnou.

* * *

He should then address the great essence, whose number *three* is contained in *one*, as well as the superior spirits, saying, Brahma! Vischnou! Siva! and you, superior Genii of the seven planets, cause the day to appear.

* * *

The second name which he should pronounce, is that of the Guru under whom he has accomplished his novitiate. He should say:

O holy Guru, I offer you my adorations and I love you as a superior spirit who has already left the world. It is through your wise lessons that I have been able to avoid evil.

* * *

He should then pray to the superior Being, to descend into his heart, saying:

Brahma is now within me, and I shall enjoy the most perfect happiness.

* * *

He should then address Vischnou, saying:

O God, who art the purest of spirits, the principle of all things, the master of the world, and the fertilizer of nature, it is by thy orders that I have left my couch and have ventured among the shoals of life.

* * *

He should then ponder over the duties of the day, and the good works and meritorious actions which it is his duty to perform.

He should remember, in order to be agreeable to the gods, that all his actions should be performed with fervor and piety, not negligently or perfunctorily.

* * *

Having set his mind upon the performance of every duty, he should then utter aloud the thousand names of Vischnou.

The Agrouchada gives the whole litany of Vischnou, which is actually composed of a thousand names. They commence as follows:

Hail to Vischnou!
Hail to Hary!
Hail to Narayana!
Hail to Covinda!
Hail to Kechva! etc.

The reader will gladly dispense with the rest.

First Part.

The Regular Ablutions.

Taking in his hand a copper vessel, he should go to some isolated place, at least an arrow's flight from his dwelling, to perform his needs.

It is impossible for us to give these singular precepts in full. They are alike among all Eastern people. We read in Deuteronomy, chapter 23, verses 12 and 13. (*Habebis locum extra castra ad quem egrediaris ad requisita naturæ, gerens paxillum in balteo; cumque sederis, fodies per circuitum, et egesta humo operies.*)

* * *

In the choice of a suitable place he should avoid the ground of a temple and the banks of a river, or a tank, a well, a much-travelled road, or a sacred wood.

He should not wear the pure cloth which he uses as a garment.

* * *

He should suspend the triple cord, which is a sign of his dignity, from his left ear.

* * *

He should stop in a place where he is sure of not being seen, and while he stays there he should not have in mind or sight, the gods, the Pitris, the ancestral shades, the sun, the moon, the seven planets, or fire, or a Brahmin, a temple, a statue of the divinity, or a woman.

* * *

He should maintain the profoundest silence.

* * *

He should chew nothing and have no burden upon his head.

* * *

Upon his departure, after washing his feet and hands in the water contained in a covered vessel, he should go to the banks of a river or tank to perform the ablution of his secret parts.

* * *

Having come to the banks of the river or tank where he proposes to purify himself, he should choose a suitable place, and a little fine sand which he should use in conjunction with the water to effect his purification.

* * *

He should know that there are several kinds of impure earths which he should not use, to wit: earth thrown up by ants, that from which the salt has been extracted, clay, the earth upon a high road, that which has been used for making lye, that which is found under a tree or in the grounds of a temple, or in a cemetery, or that which is found near holes made by rats.

* * *

He should select a fine sandy earth, free from vegetable or animal detritus of any kind.

* * *

Having provided himself with suitable earth, he should approach the water without entering it and should fill his copper vessel. If he has no vessel, he should make a hole in the sand upon the banks of a river.

* * *

Taking a handful of earth saturated with water, he should rub and wash the unclean parts three times, and his other secret parts once.

* * *

Then, after cleaning and washing himself with plenty of water, he should rinse out his mouth with the pure liquid and should swallow three mouthfuls while uttering the name of Vischnou.

* * *

In cleaning his teeth he should use a small bit of wood taken from the outanga, rengou, neradou, visouga, outara, or revanou tree or from any lacteous or thorny bushes.

* * *

Upon cutting off a branch he should address the spirits of the woods as follows:

* * *

Spirit of the forest, I cut one of these little branches to clean my teeth. Grant me, by means of the act which I am about to accomplish, a long life, strength, honors, and understanding.

Having terminated this invocation, he should cut a long stick from a palm tree, the end of which he should soften in his mouth, like a brush.

* * *

Sitting upon the edge of the water, with his face turned toward the East, he should rub all his teeth with the stick of wood and should rinse out his mouth three times with pure water.

* * *

It is not lawful for him to cleanse himself thus every day. He should abstain the sixth, eighth, ninth, eleventh, and fourteenth day of the new and full moon.

* * *

He should abstain on Tuesday of every week, and on the day presided over by the constellation beneath which he was born, as well as upon the day of the week and month corresponding to that of his birth.

* * *

He should abstain during eclipses, planetary conjunctions, equinoxes, solstices, and other inauspicious periods; upon the anniversary of his father's or mother's death he should understand that all this is absolutely forbidden.

* * *

Second Part.

Rules for General Ablutions.

Upon going to the river or tank of ablutions the Brahmin should change the water of the river or tank, by the power of the following invocation, into the sacred waters of the Ganges:

* * *

Invocation.

O Ganges, you were born from the bosom of Brahma, whence you descended upon the head of Siva and the feet of Vischnou, and came down to earth to wipe out the sins of mankind, to purify them from their uncleanness, and to obtain happiness for them; you are the refuge and stay of all animated creatures that live on this earth. I have confidence in you; take back again your holy water from this river in which I am about to perform my ablutions; in this manner you will purify my soul and body.

* * *

He should think of the spirits who preside over the sacred rivers, which are seven in number—Ganges, Yamouna, Sindou, Godavery, Sarasvatty, Nerbouda, and Cavery.

* * *

Then entering the water he should direct his attention toward the Ganges, and imagine that he is really performing his ablutions in that river.

* * *

After bathing he should turn toward the sun, and taking some water in his hands three times, he should perform an oblation to that luminary three times, letting the water drip slowly from the end of his fingers.

* * *

He should then come out of the water, gird his loins with a pure cloth, put another upon his shoulders, and sit down with his face turned toward the East, and with his copper vessel full of water standing near him: he should then rub his forehead with ground sandal-wood and trace the red mark called Tiloky, according to the practice of his caste.

* * *

He should then hang from his neck three garlands of flowers of different colors prepared by his wife, and should finish by suspending from his neck a chaplet of the red seed called Boudrakchas.

He should then think of Vischnou and should drink of the water contained in his vase three times in his honor. He should again perform three libations to the sun, pouring a little water upon the earth.

*
* *

He should perform a similar libation in honor of the celestial Trimourti—Brahma, Vischnou, Siva; and of the superior spirits—Indra, Agny, Yama, Neiritia, Varouna, Vahivou, Couverd, and Isania.

*
* *

To the air, to the ether, to the earth, to the pure fluid, Agasa, to the universal principle of force and life, and to all the Pitris and ancestral shades, uttering the names of all those which occur to his mind.

*
* *

He should then arise and pay homage to Vischnou, reciting in his honor the prayers which are most agreeable to him.

*
* *

Turning around slowly three times, he should pronounce the names of the divine Trinity, nine times at every revolution. Then uttering slowly the three names contained in the mysterious monosyllable—Brahma, Vischnou, Siva—he should make nine revolutions at each repetition thereof.

*
* *

When he pronounces the mysterious monosyllable itself in a low tone, he should rapidly make nine revolutions and recite the following invocation to the sun:

*
* *

Invocation.

O Sun! you are the eye of Brahma at day-break, the eye of Vischnou at noon, and that of Siva at evening.

You are the diamond of the Infinite, the precious stone of the air, the king of day, the witness of all actions that take place in the universe. Your warmth fertilizes nature. You are the measure of time. You regulate days, nights, weeks, months, years, cycles, calpas, yuyas, seasons, and the time for ablutions and prayer. You are the lord of the nine planets. You remove all the impurities of the globe. You scatter darkness wherever you appear. In the space of sixty gahdias you survey from your chariot the whole of the great mountain of the north, which extends for ninety millions six hundred yodjomas. I offer you my adoration, as to the superior spirit which watches over the earth.

* * *

In honor of his tutelary star and of the spirit which animates it, he then turns around twelve times, twenty-four times, or if his strength enables him twenty-four times, forty-eight times.[1]

* * *

In this manner he disciplines the body, increases his strength, and prepares himself for mysterious evocations. He then goes toward the tree, Assouata, and, after resting himself in its shade, he addresses to it the following invocation:

* * *

Invocation.

O Tree Assouata![2] you are the king of the forests and the image and symbol of the gods. Your roots represent Brahma, your trunk Vischnou, and your branches Siva; thus you represent the Trimourti. All those who honor you in this world by performing the ceremony of

[1] This is undoubtedly the origin of the Bonzes and whirling dervishes.

[2] All Brahmins plant them about their temples and dwelling-houses

imitation, by *turning* around you, and by celebrating your praises, obtain the *knowledge of things* in this world and a *superior form* in another.

* * *

He then revolves around the tree seven, fourteen, twenty-one, twenty-eight, thirty-five times and more, until his strength is exhausted, always increasing the number of revolutions by seven.

* * *

When he is rested he should engage, for a while, in devout meditation; he should then clothe himself with clean garments, and, after plucking a few flowers with which to offer sacrifices to the domestic spirits, he should return to the house, with his vessel full of water.

* * *

Third Part.

Acts after Ablutions.

Upon returning home the Grihasta performs the sacrifice to the fire and can then attend to his other duties.

* * *

At noon, after ordering his mid-day meal, he should return to the river for the purpose of repeating the sandya and of reciting the prayers which will be hereafter given in the ritual.

* * *

Then he should return home, and try to keep himself pure by carefully abstaining from touching or walking upon anything capable of contaminating him.

* * *

If he should come in contact with any person of an inferior caste, or should step upon any vegetable or animal detritus, upon any hair or bones, he should return to the river and repeat his ablutions.

* * *

He should be in a state of perfect purity in order to offer the sacrifice to the Pitris which it now becomes his office to perform.

* * *

After preparing himself for this important ceremony, he should thoughtfully enter the room in his house reserved for the domestic spirits which he is accustomed to evoke, and should engage in the ceremonies preparatory to evocation.

Evocation in the First Degree.

After darkening a part of the room he should deposit in that portion of it a vase full of water, a lamp, and some powdered sandal-wood, boiled rice, and incense.

* * *

Snapping his fingers together, and turning around upon his heels he should trace before the door the magic circles as taught him by the superior Guru, in order to prevent the entrance of any bad spirits from the outside and to confine within it any which have already penetrated to the sanctuary of the Pitris.

* * *

With earth, water, and fire, breathed upon three times, he should compose a new body for himself, and with a part of his, should form a body for the spirits which he intends to evoke for the sacrifice.

* * *

He should then compress the right nostril with his thumb and pronounce the monosyllable *Djom!* sixteen times. Breathing in strongly by his left nostril he should by degrees separate the particles of which his body is composed.

* * *

With the thumb and fore-finger he should then press both nostrils and pronounce the word *Rom!* six times. He should stop breathing and summon fire to his aid in order to disperse his body.

* * *

He should pronounce the word *Lom!* thirty-two times, when his soul will escape from his body, and his body will disappear and the soul of the spirits he has evoked will animate the new body he prepared for it.

* * *

His soul will then return to his body, the subtile parts of which will unite anew, after forming an aërial body for the spirits which he has evoked.

* * *

Pronouncing the sacred word Aum! three times and the magic syllable Djom! nine times, he should impose his hands above the lamp and throw a pinch of incense upon the flame, saying:

* * *

O sublime Pitri! O illustrious penitent narada! whom I have evoked and for whom I have formed a subtile body from the constituent particles of my own, are you present? Appear in the smoke of incense and take part in the sacrifice that I offer to the shades of my ancestors.

* * *

When he has received a suitable answer and the aërial body of the spirit evoked has appeared in the smoke of the incense, he should then proceed to perform the oblations and sacrifices as prescribed.

* * *

The sacrifices having been offered, he should hold converse with the souls of his ancestors concerning the mysteries of *being* and the transformations of the *imperishable.*

* * *

Having extinguished his lamp, in darkness and silence he should then listen to the conversation of the spirits with each other, and should be present at the manifestations by which they reveal their presence.

* * *

Lighting his lamp, he should then set at liberty the evil spirits confined in the magic circles, after which he should leave the asylum of the Pitris. It is lawful for him then to take his repast.

* * *

As soon as he has finished it, he should wash his hands, rinse his mouth twelve times, and eat nine leaves of basil, in order to facilitate his digestion.

* * *

He should distribute betel and cashew nuts to the poor whom he has invited to his table, and when they are gone he should engage for a time in the perusal of the sacred scriptures.

* * *

Having finished his reading, it is lawful for him to take some betel and to attend to his other business and to visit his friends, but he should be very careful, during every moment of his public life, never to covet the property or wife of another.

At sunset, he should return to the river to perform the ceremony of ablution, the same as in the morning.

*
* *

Upon returning to the house, he should again perform an oblation to the fire, and should recite the thousand names of the Hary-Smarana, or the litanies of Vischnou.

*
* *

He should then repair to the temple to hear the lesson given by the superior Guru to the Grihastas and Pourohitas who have passed through the first degree of initiation.

*
* *

He should never enter the temple empty handed. He should carry as a present either oil for the lamps, or cocoanuts, bananas, camphor, incense, or sandal-wood, which are used in the sacrifices. If he is poor, he should give a little betel.

*
* *

Before entering the temple he should make a circuit of it three times, and perform before the door the Schaktanga, or prostration of the six limbs.

*
* *

After hearing the lessons and taking part in the evocations of the Pitris, with the other members of his order, he should perform his devotions and return home, being careful to avoid any impurities, in order to take his evening repast, after which he should immediately lie down.

*
* *

He should never pass the night in a place consecrated to the spirits. When travelling, he should be careful not to lie down in the shadow of a tree, or in a ploughed or moist field, or in places covered with ashes, or by the edge of a cemetery.

Upon lying down he should offer his adoration to the divine Trimourti, and should recite the invocation to the spirit called Kalassa, which is agreeable to Siva.

Kalassa.

May the spirit Bahirava preserve my head from accident, the spirit Bichava my forehead; the spirit Bouta-Carma my ears; the spirit Preta-Bahava my face; the spirit Bouta-Carta my thighs; the spirits Datys (who were endowed with immense strength) my shoulders; Kalapamy my hands; Chanta my chest; Ketrica my stomach; Pattou my generative organs; Katrapala my ribs; Kebraya my mouth; Chidda-Pattou my ankles, and the superior spirit Yama my whole body. May fire, which is the essence of the life of both gods and men, preserve me from all harm, wherever I may be. May the wives of these spirits watch over my children, my cows, my horses, and my elephants; may Vischnou watch over my native land.

May God, who sees all things, watch over my family and everything else, and also watch over me, when I am in any place which is not under the care of any divinity.

* * *

He should conclude by the invocation to Brahma, the lord of creatures.

* * *

Invocation to Brahma.

O Brahma! what is this mystery which is repeated every night after the labors of the day are over, and every one has returned from the fields, and the flocks are all in their folds, and the evening repast is over?

* * *

Behold, every one lies down upon his mat and closes his eyes, and the whole body ceases to exist, and is abandoned by the soul in order that it may hold converse with the soul of its ancestors.

* * *

Watch over it, O Brahma! when, forsaking the body, which is asleep, it floats hither and thither upon the waters, or wanders through the immensities of the heavens, or penetrates the dark and mysterious recesses of the valleys and forest of Hymavat.

* * *

O Brahma! God all-powerful, who commandest the storms, the God of light and darkness, let my soul not forget, after its wanderings, to return in the morning, to animate my body and remind me of thee.

* * *

He should then stretch himself upon his mat and go to sleep. Beneficent spirits will watch over his repose. (Agrouchada-Parikchai.)

CHAPTER VI.

THE FIRST DEGREE OF INITIATION.—(*Continued.*)

Morning, Noon, and Evening Sandyas.[1]

When ten years have been spent in the first degree of initiation and there still remains an equal period of time before the Grihastas and Pourohitas can become Sannyassis and Vanaprasthas, or, in other words, can arrive at the second degree of initiation, many prayers must be added to the morning, noon, and evening ceremonies of ablution.

When he has reached this period of his life the candidate is no longer his own master. He spends almost all of his time in prayers, fastings, and in mortifications of every description. His nights are partly devoted to ceremonies of evocation in the temple under the direction of the superior Guru. He eats only once a day, after sunset. All the occult forces are put in operation to modify his physiological organization and give his powers a special direction. Few Brahmins ever arrive at the second degree of initiation. The mysterious and terrible phenomena which they produce cannot be put in operation without the exercise of a supernatural power, which very few are enabled to master.

Most Brahmins, therefore, never get beyond the class of Grihastas and Pourohitas. We shall see, however, when we have finished with the prayer and external formula, the object of which is to discipline the intellect by the daily repetition of the same acts, and when we approach

[1] Translated from the Agrouchada-Parikchai.

the subject of the manifestations and phenomena, which the initiates of the first degree claim to perform (a claim which is apparently well founded), that their faculties have been developed to a degree which has never been equalled in Europe.

As for those who belong to the second, and particularly the third classes, they claim that time and space are unknown to them, and that they have command over man and death.

* * * * * *

The following are the prayers which, during the second period of ten years of the first degree of initiation, are to be added to the ceremonies and invocations previously prescribed as acts of intellectual discipline intended to prevent the subject from remaining for a single instant under the influence of his own thoughts.

* * * * * *

The evocations which we give below are met with, with slight deviations, in all the dialects of India, and are claimed by religious sects. They are also in strict conformity with the rite of the Yadjour-Veda.

The Morning Sandya.

At the end of ten years and during the ensuing ten years, if he feels strong enough to attain the *imperishable*, the Grihasta should recite the following prayers at his morning ablutions, in addition to those already prescribed.

* * *

He should commence all his exercises by the following evocation:

> Apavitraha, pavitraha sarva vastam.
> Gatopiva yasmaret pounkarikakchan.
> Sabahiabhiam tara souchihy.

The man who is pure or impure, or who is in a perilous situation, whatever it may be, has only to invoke him whose eyes are of the same color as the lotus (pond lily) to be pure internally as well as externally, and to be saved.

He should continue by the invocation to the water:

Invocation to the Water.

O Water! consecrated by the five perfumes and by prayer, thou art pure, whether taken from the sea, from rivers, from tanks, or from well ; purify thou my body from all uncleanness.

* * *

As the traveller, weary with the heat, finds relief in the shade of a tree, so may I find in the sacred water relief from every ill and purification from all my sins.

* * *

O consecrated water! thou art the essence of sacrifice and germ of life. In thy bosom all germs have been begotten, all beings have been formed.

* * *

I invoke thee with the confidence of a child who, at the appearance of danger, rushes into the arms of his mother, who loves him tenderly. Purify me from my faults and purify all men with me.

* * *

O water! consecrated at the time of the pralaya-chao—Brahma, or the supreme wisdom—Swayambhouva, or the being existing by his own strength, dwelt under thy form. Thou wert confounded with him.

* * *

He suddenly appeared upon the vast billows which ruffled the surface of infinite space and created a form in which he revealed himself and separated the land from the waters, which when assembled together in one spot form the vast ocean.

* * *

The unrevealed being, Brahma, who seated on the waves of the vast ether, drew from his own substance the three-faced Trimourti, which created the heavens and the earth, the air, and all the inferior worlds.

* * *

Upon terminating, he should sprinkle a few drops of water upon his head with three stalks of the sacred darba grass.

* * *

He who addresses this invocation to the water at morning, and who is thoroughly penetrated with its mystic meaning, has arrived at a high degree of sanctity.

* * *

Joining then his hands, he should say, "O Vischnou! I do this to preserve my dignity as a Grihasta."

* * *

He should then think of the superior and inferior worlds, of the spirits which inhabit them, of the spirits of the fire, of the wind, of the sun, and of all the spirits of the earth.

* * *

Raising his hand to his head, he should then call to mind all the names of Brahma, and closing his eyes, and compressing his nostrils, he should perform the evocation of that God, as follows.

* * *

Come, Brahma! come down to my bosom.

* * *

He should then figure to himself this supreme deity as

having had no beginning and as possessing all knowledge, like the Guru, the eternal principle of all things.

* * *

And he should say, Hail Brahma! thou who art the essence of everything that exists, of water, of fire, of air, of the ether, of space, and of infinity: I offer thee my adoration.

* * *

He should then evoke Vischnou, and should figure him to himself as emerging from the bosom of the water in the midst of a lotus flower.

* * *

He should then evoke Siva, saying, You who destroy and transform everything, destroy and transform everything that is impure in me.

* * *

The Grihasta should then address the following prayer to the Sun.

Invocation to the Sun.

O Sun! whose fire purifies everything, and who art the spirit of prayer, purify me from the faults which I have committed in my prayers and sacrifices, from all those which I have committed at night in thought or action, from those which I have committed against my neighbor by calumny, false witness, or coveting another's wife, by eating prohibited food, at unlawful hours, or by communication with vile men, and finally from all the impurities which I may have contracted, whether during the day or during the night.

* * *

O Sun! you give birth to fire and it is from you that the spirits receive those subtile particles which unite to form their aërial bodies.

He should trace around him the magic circles which prevent evil spirits from approaching him.

* * *

Addressing the immortal Goddess, Nari, who is an emblem of nature in the Hindu mythology, he should then express himself in the following terms.

* * *

O illustrious Goddess! I pay homage to you; grant that when I lay aside presently this perishable envelope I may rise to higher spheres.

* * *

Placing then both hands above the copper vessel filled with water, he should then evoke the son of Kasiappa, or any other sage of past time, asking him to listen to the praises that he addresses to Nari and to recite them with him.

* * *

The spirit having appeared he should repeat in a loud voice the following words, in honor of the universal mother.

* * *

Invocation to Nari.

O divine spouse of him who moves upon the waters, preserve me, both during the day and during the night.

You are of a spiritual nature.
You are the light of lights.
You are not subject to human passions.
You are eternal.
You are all-powerful.
You are purity itself.
You are the refuge of men.
You are their salvation.
You are *knowledge*.

You are the essence of the sacred scriptures.
By your constant fruitfulness the universe is sustained.
You are the figure of evocation.
You are prayer.
To you all sacrifices should be addressed.
You are the dispenser of every good.
Everything is in your hands; joy, sorrow, fear, hope.
You are present in the three worlds.
You have three figures.
The number three forms your essence.

* * *

Nari, the immortal virgin.
Brahmy, the universal mother.
Hyranya, the golden matrix.
Paramatma, the soul of all beings.
Sakty, the Queen of the universe.
Lakny, the celestial light.
Mariama, perpetual fruitfulness.
Agasa, the pure fluid.
Ahancara, the supreme conscience.
Conya, the chaste virgin.
Tanmatra, the union of the five elements: Air, fire, water, earth, ether.
Trigana, virtue, riches, love.
Conyabava, eternal virginity.

* * *

He should then make a vow to recite this sublime invocation, which is a source of all life and all transformation, at least three times a day.

Noon Sandya.

He should repeat the same prayers after the noon ablutions, and should perform the evocation of spirits by water.

Midnight Sandya.

Having offered the sacrifice to fire, he should then evoke the spirits of night, in the smoke of incense, saying:

Spirits of the waters,
Spirits of the forests,
Spirits of unfrequented roads,
Spirits of public places,
Spirits of sandy plains,
Spirits of the jungles,
Spirits of the mountains,
Spirits of burial places,
Spirits of the ocean,
Spirits of the wind,
Spirits of the tempest,
Destructive spirits,
Ensnaring spirits,
Spirits of salt deserts,
Spirits of the East,
Spirits of the West,
Spirits of the North,
Spirits of the South,
Spirits of darkness,
Spirits of bottomless gulfs,
Spirits of heaven,
Spirits of the earth,
Spirits of hell,

Come all and listen, bear these words in mind.

* * *

Protect all travellers, and caravans, all men who work. who suffer, who pray, or who rest, all those who, in the silence of night, carry dead bodies to the funeral pyre, those who travel deserts, or forests, or the vast ocean.

* * *

O spirits, come and listen. Bear these words in mind and protect all men. (Agrouchada-Parikchai.)

CHAPTER VII.

THE SECOND DEGREE OF INITIATION.

Having spent twenty years of his life after receiving the first degree of initiation, during which the body is mortified by fasting and privations of every kind, and the intellect is trained and disciplined by means of prayers, invocations, and sacrifices, the candidate finally takes his place in one of the three following categories:

Grihasta—he remains at the head of his family until his death, and attends to his social duties and business, whatever it may be. Of all that he has been taught he only retains the power to evoke the domestic spirits, or in other words, those in the same genealogical line as himself, with whom it is lawful for him to communicate within the sanctuary which it is his duty to reserve for them in his house.

Pourohita—he becomes a priest attached to the popular cult and takes part in all ceremonies and family festivals, both in temples and private dwellings. Phenomena of possession come exclusively within his province: he is the grand exorcist of the pagodas.

Fakir—he becomes a performing Fakir, and from this moment forward all his time is employed in the manifestation of occult power by means of the public exhibition of exterior phenomena.

Neither Grihastas, Pourohitas, nor Fakirs are ever admitted to the second degree of initiation. Their studies are ended, and with the exception of the Fakirs, who are constantly in communication with those who have been initiated into the higher degrees, in order to augment their magnetic and spiritual power, they take no part in the mystic instruction, which is given in the temples.

Only a few among those who have distinguished themselves in their studies for the first degree are able to pass through the terrible ordeal of the higher initiation or arrive at the dignity of a Sannyassi or Cenobite.

The Sannyassi lives exclusively in the temple, and he is only expected to appear at remote intervals, on solemn occasions, in cases where it is important to impress the popular imagination by a superior class of phenomena.

The Agrouchada-Parikchai is silent as to the course of training they have to undergo. The formulas of prayer and evocation were never committed to writing, but were taught orally, in the underground crypts of the pagodas.

We are able therefore to prosecute our investigations into the subject of the second degree of initiation only by studying the phenomena produced by the Sannyassi, a list of which we find in the second book of the Agrouchada.

CHAPTER VIII.

THE THIRD DEGREE OF INITIATION.

It is not until he has spent a further period of twenty years in the study of the occult sciences and manifestations that the Sannyassi becomes a Sannyassi-Nirvany or Naked Cenobite, so called because he was not to wear any garments whatever, thus indicating that he had broken the last tie that bound him to the earth. We are limited to such means of information as are obtainable by the uninitiated. The book of the Pitris, or spirits, which is our guide in this inquiry, contains no explanation with regard to the mysterious occupations in which the Sannyassis-Nirvanys, who have been initiated in the third degree, engage. The chapter devoted to this subject merely gives the following magical words, of which the Brahmins would furnish us no explanation whatever, which were inscribed in two triangles. They were:

L'om	Sho'rhim
L'rhom-sh'hrum.	Ramaya-namaha.

We can only study the subject of the highest initiation in its philosophical teachings regarding God and man. The phenomena performed by the Nirvanys are not described in the book of Pitris.

We have not been able to glean much from private conversations with Pourohitas, with regard to the actions of their superiors. It seems that they live in a constant state of ecstatic contemplation, depriving themselves of sleep as far as possible, and taking food only once a week, after sunset.

They are never visible either in the grounds or inside the temples, except on the occasion of the grand festival of fire, which occurs every five years. On that day they appear at midnight upon a stand erected in the centre of the sacred tank. They appear like spectres, and the surrounding atmosphere is illumined by them by means of their incantations. They seem to be in the midst of a column of light rising from earth to heaven.

The air is filled with strange sounds, and the five or six hundred thousand Hindus who have come from all parts of India to see these demi-gods, as they are esteemed, prostrate themselves flat in the dust, calling upon the souls of their ancestors.

CHAPTER IX.

THE GRAND COUNCIL.

In the present chapter we will merely give a few verses from the Agrouchada-Parikchai treating of the Supreme Council.

* * *

"Seventy Brahmins more than seventy years old are chosen from among the Nirvanys to see that the *law of the Lotus*, or the occult science, is never revealed to the vulgar, and that those who have been initiated into the sacred order are not contaminated by the admission of any unworthy person."

* * *

None should be chosen unless they have always practised the ten virtues, in which, according to the divine Manu, the performance of duty consists.

* * *

Resignation, *the action of returning good for evil*, temperance, probity, purity, chastity, the subjugation of the senses, a knowledge of the sacred scriptures, that of the supreme soul, the worship of the truth, abstinence from anger—such are the principles which should be the rule of conduct of a true Nirvany.

* * *

He who is called to rule over others should first yield obedience to all the precepts of the sacred books.

He should not desire death; he should not desire life; like the reaper who patiently waits at evening for his wages at his master's door, he should wait till his time has come.

* * *

He should purify his steps by taking heed where he sets his foot; he should purify the water he drinks, in order that he may not cause the death of any animal; he should purify his words by truth; he should purify his soul by virtue.

* * *

He should endure bad language, insults, and blows patiently, without returning them; he should carefully avoid cherishing ill-will against any person on account of anything connected with this miserable body.

* * *

Meditating upon the delights of the supreme soul, needing nothing, beyond the reach of any sensual desire, with no society save his own soul and the thought of God, he should live here below in the constant expectation of everlasting happiness.

* * *

He should never resort to places frequented by Grihastas or Pourohitas, unless they have entirely renounced the world. (Manu.)

* * *

He should avoid all meetings, even when Brahmins alone are present. He should be careful, as he regards his eternal salvation, not to resort to places used for bird or dog fights.

* * *

A wooden platter, a gourd, an earthern vessel, and a bamboo basket—such are the pure utensils authorized by Manu; he should keep nothing in the precious metals.

He should reflect that the vital spirit, after leaving the Great All, undergoes ten thousand million transformations, before clothing itself with a human form.

* * *

He should observe the incalculable ills which grow out of the practice of iniquity, and the great happiness that springs from the practice of virtue.

* * *

He should bear constantly in mind the perfections and invisible essences of a Paramatma, the great soul, which is present in all bodies, the lowest as well as the highest.

* * *

He should know that an atom is an exact representation of the Great All.

* * *

The Nirvany should expiate his faults by solitary reflection, by meditation, by the repression of every sensual desire, by meritorious austerity; he should destroy all the imperfections of his nature that may be opposed to the divine nature.

* * *

Such is the rule of conduct by which those Sannyassis-Nirvanys are governed who aspire to enter the Supreme Council. It possesses the largest disciplinary powers in order to prevent the divulgation of the mysteries of initiation.

The following are some of the terrible penalties it is commanded to inflict.

* * *

Whoever has been initiated, no matter what may be the degree to which he may belong, and shall reveal the sacred formula, shall be put to death.

Whoever has been initiated into the third degree and shall reveal the superior truths he has been taught, to the candidates for initiation into the second degree before the proper time, shall suffer death.

* * *

Whoever has been initiated into the second degree and shall act likewise with those who have been initiated into the first degree, is declared impure for the period of seven years, and when that time has elapsed, he shall be turned back to the lower class (the first degree).

* * *

Whoever has been initiated into the first degree, and shall divulge the secrets of his initiation to the members of the other castes, who are forever debarred from knowing them, as though they were contained in a sealed book, shall be deprived of sight, and after his tongue and both hands have been cut off, in order that he may not make an improper use of what he has learned, he shall be expelled from the temple, as well as from his caste.

* * *

Any one belonging to the three lower castes, who shall gain admission to the secret asylums, or shall surreptitiously acquire a knowledge of the formula of evocation, shall be burned to death.

* * *

If a virgin should do so, she shall be confined in the temple and consecrated to the worship of fire. (Agrouchada-Parikchai.)

In addition to its attributes as an initiatory tribunal, the council of the elders also had charge of administering the pagoda property, from which it made provision for the wants of its members, of the three classes, who lived entirely in common. It also directed the wanderings of the Fakirs, who have charge of the exterior manifestations of occult power.

* * *

The Brahmatma was elected by it from its own number.

CHAPTER X.

THE ELECTION OF THE BRAHMATMA.

I have not much to add to what I have already said about the Brahmatma.

The requisite qualifications for the position were that the candidate should have been initiated, that he should have taken the vow of chastity, and that he should be a member of the Supreme Council.

That this vow was a serious matter will be readily understood when it is known that any Brahmin taking it in the commencement of his career must necessarily persevere until he arrives at the dignity of Yoguy, unless he wishes to repeat upon earth a series of transformations. Not having paid the *debt of his ancestors*, by the birth of a son, who can continue his genealogical line and officiate at his funeral, he would be obliged to come back after death, under a new human envelope, to accomplish that final duty.

The Yoguys, or members of the Council of Seventy, by reason of their high degree of sanctity, had no new transmigrations to undergo: it was a matter of indifference whether they had been heads of families or whether they had always maintained their chastity. But in view of the small number admitted into this sanhedrim, if we may so call it, the Brahmin who should pronounce this terrible vow, as it is termed in the book of the Pitris, at the close of his novitiate, was in danger of having to go through a succession of new lives, from the first monad, by which the smallest particle of moss is animated, to man, who is, so far, the most perfect expression of the vital form.

While the Brahmatma could only be chosen from among those Yoguys who had taken the vow of chastity, his election was not due to any supposed degree of sanctity on his part resulting therefrom, for he had hardly been elected, when, notwithstanding his advanced age of eighty years, in order that his election might be held valid, he had to furnish evidence of his virile power in connection with one of the virgins of the Pagoda, who was given him as a bride.

If a male child sprang from this union he was placed in a wicker basket, and turned adrift upon the river to float with the current. If perchance he was washed ashore he was carried to the temple, where he was at once, and by virtue of that very fact, regarded as having been initiated into the third degree. From his earliest childhood, all the secret mentrams, or formulas of evocation, were made known to him.

If, however, the child floated down the stream with the current, he was rejected as a Pariah, and handed over to the people of that caste to be reared by them.

We never could discover the origin of this singular custom. Upon comparing other ancient usages with the manners and customs of the sacerdotal castes in Egypt, which are so similar in many respects to those of the Indian temples, we have often asked ourselves the following questions, which we now propound for the reader's consideration:

Might not Moses, the leader of the Hebraic revolution, have been a son of the Egyptian high priest, who stood at the head of the order of the initiated, and might he not have been brought to the temple, because he had been cast ashore by the Nile?

Might not his brother Aaron, on the contrary, have been cast aside as one of the servile class, because when he was set adrift likewise upon the river he floated along with the current without being cast ashore?

May we not regard the friendship of the two brothers for each other, when informed subsequently of their common origin, as one of the causes that impelled Moses to abandon the sacerdotal caste, of which he was a member, in order to place himself at the head of the Egyptian slaves, and lead them into the desert in search of that promised land which the pariahs, helots, and outcasts of every degree have always looked forward to in their dreams as the sunny land of peace and liberty?

We suggest the question, however, we repeat, merely as a supposition. Perhaps ethnographic science, by which the second half of the present century has been so brilliantly illustrated, will show, some day, that it is something more.

CHAPTER XI.

THE YOGUYS.

Previous to a more thorough investigation into the doctrine of the Pitris, and the external manifestations by whose aid the Hindus attempt to prove the existence of an occult power, we have a few words further to say about the Yoguys.

Although none but those who had passed through the third degree of initiation and were consequently members of the Council of the Elders, and who had always abstained from carnal intercourse, ever attained the degree of Yoguy, it was, says the Book of Spirits, a state so sublime that those who were versed in its mysteries were entitled to a greater degree of merit during their lives than most men could acquire during ten million new generations and transmigrations.

"The Yoguy is as much superior to those who have gone through the highest degree of initiation, as spirits are superior to men."

"A passing feeling of spite or enthusiasm," says the Agrouchada-Parikchai, "should never induce a Brahmin to take the vow of chastity. His vocation should be the well-considered result of careful examination, and its motive should be, not the ambition to rise to the highest dignities, but a feeling of disgust with the world and its pleasures, and an ardent desire to arrive at perfection."

He should feel as though he could readily dispense with all earthly pleasures of whatever kind or degree. If he still cherished, in his inmost heart, the slightest hankering for those treasures that others esteem so highly, and strive for so ardently, that alone was quite enough to counterbalance any advantage or benefit that he might otherwise have derived from his penitence.

When the Brahmatchary has ended his novitiate and has fully considered his future course, he repairs to a meeting consisting of all the initiates and informs them of his determination. He asks them to proceed with the usual forms and ceremonies, to the reception of the momentous vows he desires to pronounce.

On the day appointed for this solemn act the candidate first purifies himself by ablutions: he then provides himself with ten pieces of cloth large enough to cover his shoulders. Four of these are intended for his own use, while the other six are given as presents to the officiating Pourohitas.

The chief Guru who presides at the ceremony, hands him a bamboo stick containing seven joints, some lotus flowers, and powdered sandal-wood, and whispers in his ear certain mentrams of evocation, which are only made known to persons in his condition.

This stick is not intended to help support his steps or to be of any assistance to him in walking. It is the magic wand used in divination and all the occult phenomena.

It is involuntarily suggestive of the rod of Moses, Aaron, Elisha, and all the prophets, of the augural wand, and of the seven-knotted wand of the Fauns, Sylvans, and Cynics.

When the ceremony is finished, the Yoguy takes up his magic wand, a calabash for drinking purposes, and a gazelle's skin, to be used as a bed. These articles comprise his whole store, and he never leaves them; they are the *omnium mecum porto* of the Stoics. He then departs, repeating the magical formulas which he has just learned from the superior Guru.

In addition to the usual ablutions, ceremonies, and

prayers, which he has to perform, like all who have been initiated, the following prescriptions are imposed upon him.

* * *

"Every morning after performing his ablutions he should smear his entire body with ashes; others only rubbed their foreheads. Christianity still retains a symbolic remnant of this ceremony—*homo pulvis es*, etc.

"He should only eat daily, after sunset, as much rice as he can hold in the hollow of his hand.

"He should abandon the use of betel.

"He should avoid the company of women and he should not even look at them.

"Once a month he should have his head and face shaved.

"He should wear only wooden sandals.

"He should live by alms."

"Although a Yoguy," says the work to which we have referred as our guide, "has the right to demand alms, it is more becoming for him to receive them without asking. Consequently, when he is hungry, he should present himself among this world's people, without saying anything or telling them what he wants. If anything is given to him voluntarily, he should receive it with an air of indifference, and without expressing his thanks. If nothing is offered, he should withdraw quietly, without expressing anger or dissatisfaction; neither should he make any complaint if anything that is given him is not to his taste."

"He should not sit down to eat.

"He should build a hermitage by the side of a river or tank, in order that he may perform his ablutions with greater facility."

"When travelling, he should abide nowhere, and should only pass through populous places.

"He should look at all men alike, and should regard himself as superior to anything that may happen. He should look upon the various revolutions by which the world is agitated and powerful empires are sometimes overturned, as matters of perfect indifference to him."

"His only care should be to acquire the spirit of wisdom, and that degree of spirituality by means of which he will finally be reunited to the Divinity, from whom all creatures and passions tend to keep us apart. In order to accomplish that object, he should have his senses under the most perfect control, and entirely subdue the sentiments of anger, envy, avarice, lust, and all disturbing and licentious thoughts. Otherwise he will derive no benefit whatever from having taken the vow or from his repeated mortifications."

Every evening, the Yoguy repairs to the pagoda, with his magic wand, his calabash, and his gazelle's skin, where he passes several hours in contemplation in the most profound darkness. He there endeavors to accustom his soul to forsake his body, in order that it may hold converse with the Pitris in infinite space. He ends the night with the study of manifestations and incantations, in which he is further instructed by the superior Guru.

When, in his eightieth year, in consequence of his superior sanctity, or for some other reason, he has been chosen by the Council for the post of Brahmatma, he goes back again, so to speak, to life, and spends his last years in the most unbridled indulgence and dissipation. We have often heard the Brahmins say, though we have had no opportunity to verify their statements, that, in consequence of their long practice of asceticism, the Yoguys often preserved all the virile powers of mature age until far advanced in life, and it was no unusual thing for Brahmatmas to live much more than a hundred years, and leave behind them a numerous progeny.

We have now concluded these brief notices with regard to those who have passed through the various degrees of initiation. It was necessary that we should give them, in order that our main subject might be more fully understood. Though some of the details are rather dry, we hope that our readers will give them their careful attention. They are essential to the proper understanding of what is to follow.

One word more, however, about the Yoguy's seven-knotted stick.

There is a certain degree of sacredness attending the number seven in India. We may judge of the veneration in which it is held by the Brahmins, by the many objects and places the number of which is always divisible by seven, to which they attach an extraordinary magical power.

Some of them are as follows:

Sapta-Richis, the seven sages of India.

Sapta-Poura, the seven celestial cities.

Sapta-Douipa, the seven sacred islands.

Sapta-Samoudra, the seven oceans.

Sapta-Nady, the seven sacred rivers.

Sapta-Parvatta, the seven holy mountains.

Sapta-Arania, the seven sacred deserts.

Sapta-Vrukcha, the seven celestial trees.

Sapta-Coula, the seven castes.

Sapta-Loca, the seven superior and inferior worlds, etc.

According to the Brahmins, the mystical meaning of the number *seven* contains an allegorical representation of the unrevealed God, the initial trinity, and the manifested trinity; thus:

Zyans
(The Unrevealed God).
The immortal germ of everything that exists.
The initial trinity,
Nara—Nari—Viradj.

Zyans, having divided his body into two parts, male and female, or Nara and Nari, produced Viradj, the Word, the Creator,

The manifested trinity,
Brahma—Vischnou—Siva.

The initial trinity, which was purely creative, changed into the manifested trinity, as soon as the universe had come out of chaos, in order to create perpetually, to preserve eternally, and to consume unceasingly.

We should not forget that the Jews also attached a mystical meaning to the number seven, which shows indisputably its origin.

According to the Bible:

The world was created in seven days.

Land should rest every seven years.

The Sabbatic year of jubilee returned every seven times seven years.

The great golden candlestick in the temple had seven branches, the seven candles of which represented the seven planets.

Seven trumpets were blown by seven priests for seven successive days around Jericho, and the walls of that city fell down on the seventh day after the Israelitish army had marched round it for the seventh time.

In John's Apocalypse, we find:

The seven churches.

The seven chandeliers.

The seven stars.

The seven lamps.

The seven seals.

The seven angels.

The seven vials.

The seven plagues.

In like manner, the Prophet Isaiah, desiring to give an idea of the glory surrounding Jehovah, says:

"That it is seven times greater than that of the sun, and equal to the light of seven days combined."

We shall now see in how many points and how closely, the Jewish Cabala and the Hindu doctrine of the Pitris, resemble each other.

SECOND PART.

THE PHILOSOPHICAL TENETS OF THE INDIAN INITIATES.

REGARDING THE FIRST CAUSE, AND THE PART PERFORMED BY THE SPIRITS IN WORLDLY MATTERS.

Regarding the ten Pradjapatis, or lords of creatures, who are Maritchi — Atri — Augiras — Poulastya — Poulaha — Cratou — Pratchetas— Vasichta—Brighou—Narada, they have no beginning, nor end, nor time, nor space, for they proceed, from the sole essence of the one spirit, at a single breath. This is a fatal secret, close thy mouth in order that no part of it may be revealed to the rabble, and compress thy brain so that none of it may get abroad. (Agrouchada-Parikchai, "The Book of the Pitris.")

THE PHILOSOPHICAL DOCTRINES

OF THE

INDIAN INITIATES.

CHAPTER I.

THE DEGREE OF SANCTITY WHICH THE INITIATES MUST HAVE ATTAINED BEFORE RECEIVING THE SACRED FORMULA AND THE FATAL SECRET.

In order that there may be no misunderstanding as to our meaning, we will now define the different attributes of those who had been admitted to the various degrees of initiation.

It appears from what we have already ascertained:

First, that those who had been admitted into the first degree of initiation were subjected to a course of treatment, which was designed to subdue their will and enslave their intellect, and by fasting, mortifications, privations of every kind, and violent exercises in the same circuit, to change, so to speak, the direction of their physiological faculties. The outward manifestation of occult power was the utmost limit of the attainments of this class of Brahmins.

Second, that those who had been initiated into the second degree went but one step further in the line of evocations and external phenomena, and, while they exhibited the highest expression of manifested power, they never arrived at the degree of philosophical initiation.

Third, that those who were initiated into the third degree (the Sanyassis-Nirvanys and Yoguys) alone were admitted to a knowledge of the formulas behind which the highest metaphysical speculations were hidden.

The principal duty of persons of that class, was to arrive at a complete forgetfulness of all worldly matters.

The sages of India compared the passions to those heavy clouds which sometimes shut out the view of the sun entirely, or obscure the brilliancy of its light; to a violent wind, which agitates the surface of the water so that it cannot reflect the splendor of the vault above; to the envelope of the chrysalis, which deprives it of liberty; to the shell of certain fruits, which prevent their fragrance from diffusing itself abroad.

Yet, say they, the chrysalis gnaws through its envelope, makes itself a passage, and wings its way into space, thus conquering air, light, and liberty.

"So it is with the soul," says the Agrouchada. "Its prison in the body in which earthly troubles and tumultuous passions keep it confined, is not eternal. After a long series of successive births, the spark of wisdom which is in it being rekindled, it will finally succeed, by the long-continued practice of penitence and contemplation, in breaking all the ties that bind it to the earth, and will increase in virtue until it has reached so high a degree of wisdom and spirituality, that it becomes identified with the divinity. Then leaving the body, which holds it captive, its soars freely aloft, where it unites forever with the first principle, from which it originally emanated."

Having reached the third degree of initiation, it is the duty of the Brahmin to improve, to spiritualize himself by contemplation; he was supposed to pass through the four following states:

First, Salokiam.

Second, Samipiam.
Third, Souaroupiam.
Fourth, Sayodjyam.

Salokiam signifies *the only tie.* In this state the soul seeks to lift itself in thought to the celestial mansion, and to take its place in the presence of divinity itself; it holds converse with the Pitris who have gone before into the regions of everlasting life, and makes use of the body as an unconscious instrument to transcribe, under the permanent form of writing, the sublime teachings it may have received from the shades of its ancestors.

Samipiam signifies *proximity.* By the exercise of contemplation and the disregard of all earthly objects, the knowledge and idea of God become more familiar to it. The soul seems to draw nearer to him. It becomes far-seeing and begins to witness marvels, which are not of this world.

Souaroupiam signifies *resemblance.* In the third state the soul gradually acquires a perfect resemblance to the divinity, and participates in all its attributes. It reads the future, and the universe has no secrets for it.

Sayodjyam signifies *identity.* The soul finally becomes closely united to the great soul. This last transformation takes place only through death, that is to say, the entire disruption of all material ties.

The work which we are now analyzing explains the passage of the soul through these four states by the following comparison:

"When we wish to extract the gold from a compound mass, we shall never succeed if we subject it to the process of fusion only once. It is only by melting the alloy in the crucible several times, that we are finally able to separate the heterogeneous particles of which it is composed, and release the gold in all its purity."

The two modes of contemplation most in use, are called Sabda-Brahma and Sabda-Vischnou, or intercourse with Brahma and Vischnou.

It is by fasting and prayer in the forest and jungles, among the wild beasts, whom they rule by the power of the pure agasa fluid, and upon the desert banks of torrents, that the Nirvanys (naked) and the Yoguys (contemplative) prepare themselves for these lofty meditations.

There have been critical periods in the history of India, when the members of the sacerdotal caste were called upon to strike a decisive blow, in order to bring the people back to their duty and reduce them to submission. At such times they came flocking in from their habitations in the deserts, or their sombre haunts in the interiors of the temples, to preach to the masses the duty of obedience and self-renunciation.

They were accompanied by tigers and panthers, which were as gentle and submissive as so many lambs, and they performed the most extraordinary phenomena, causing rivers to overflow their banks, the light of the sun to pale, or words denouncing the Rajahs who persecuted the Brahmins to appear upon the walls of their palaces, through some unknown power.

The study of philosophic truth does not relieve them from the necessity of the tapassas, or bodily mortifications. On the contrary, it would seem that they carry them to the greatest extremes.

Once a week some sit naked in the centre of a circle formed by four blazing fires which are constantly fed by neophytes.

Others cause themselves to be buried up to their necks in the hot sand, leaving their bare skulls exposed to the blazing sun.

Others still stand upon one foot until the leg is swollen and covered with ulcers.

Everything that affects or consumes the body, everything that tends to its annihilation, without actually destroying it, is thought to be meritorious.

Every evening, the Nirvanys and Yoguys lay aside their

exercises and studies at sunset, and go into the country to meditate.

Several centuries previous to the present era, however, these bodily mortifications had assumed a character of unusual severity.

To the contemplative dreamers of the earliest ages in India, who devoted the whole of their time to meditation, and never engaged in practices involving physical suffering oftener than once a week, had succeeded a class of bigoted fanatics, who placed no limit to their religious enthusiasm, and inflicted upon themselves the most terrible tortures.

A spiritual reaction, however, occurred, and those who had been initiated into the higher degrees took that opportunity to abandon the practice of the tapassas, or corporal mortification. They sought rather to impress the imagination of the people by excessive severity in opposition to the laws of nature. A profound humility, an ardent desire to live unknown by the world, and to have the divinity as the only witness to the purity of their morals, took possession of them, and though they continued the practice of excessive abstemiousness, they did so perhaps more that they might not seem to be in conflict with the formal teachings of the sacred scriptures.

That kind of austerity is the only one now enjoined upon all classes of initiates.

The Fakirs appear to have gradually monopolized all the old modes of inflicting pain, and have carried them to the greatest extremes. They display the most unbounded fanaticism in their self-inflicted tortures upon all great public festivals.

Ever since the temporal power of the Brahmins was overthrown, the higher class of initiates have been, in short, nothing more than cenobites, or hermits, who, either in the desert or in the subterranean crypts of the temples, spend their lives in contemplation, prayer, sacrifice, the study of the most elevated philosophical problems, and the evocation of spirits, whom they regard as intermediate beings between God and man.

The spirits with whom they communicate are the shades of holy personages, who have quit the world after leading a life of privation, good works, and virtuous example: they are the objects of a regular worship, and are invoked as the spiritual directors of their brethren, who are still bound by the ties of their earthly existence.

The earliest Christians with their apparitions, their apostles who received the gift of tongues, their thaumaturgists, and their exorcists, only continued a tradition which has existed from the earliest times without interruption. There is no difference between the disciples of Peter and Paul and the initiates of India, between the saints of the Christianity of the Catacombs and the Pitris of the Brahmins.

Subsequently, the chiefs, in the interest of their temporal and religious domination, discouraged both the belief and practice, and, by slow degrees, the old system of ancient worship assumed the more modern form with which we are familiar.

It was not until they had passed through the first three of the contemplative states to which we have alluded that the Nirvanys and Yoguys were admitted to a knowlegde of the higher philosophical studies, and they were thus made acquainted with the secrets of human destiny, both present and future.

When he who had been initiated into the third degree had passed the age of eighty, and was not a member of the Supreme Council, who all remained in active life until their death, he was supposed to have abandoned his pagoda, or the hermitage that he occupied, to have renounced all pious practices, ceremonies, sacrifices, and evocations, and to have retired to some lonely and uninhabited spot, there to await the coming of death. He no longer received food or nourishment, except by chance, and passed away in the contemplation of the infinite.

* * *

"Having abandoned all his duties," says Manu, "and relinquished the direction of the sacrifices and the performance of the five ablutions, having wiped away all his faults by the prescribed purifications, having curbed all his organs and mastered the vedas to their fullest extent, he should refer all ceremonies and the offering of the funeral repast to his son for performance."

* * *

Having thus abandoned every religious observance, every act of austere devotion, applying his mind solely to the contemplation of the great first cause, exempt from every evil desire, his soul already stands at the threshold of swarga, although his mortal envelope still palpitates and flutters like the last flames of an expiring lamp.

CHAPTER II.

THE SUPERIOR GURU—THE SACRED DECADE.

Upon reaching the third degree of initiation, the Brahmins were divided into tens, and a superior Guru, or professor of the occult sciences, was placed over each decade. He was revered by his disciples as a god.

The following is a portrait of this personage, as drawn in the *Védanta-sara:*

"The true Guru is a man who is familiar with the practice of every virtue; who, with the sword of wisdom, has lopped off all the branches and cut through all the roots of the tree of evil, and, with the light of reason, has dispelled the thick darkness by which he is enveloped; who, though seated upon a mountain of passions, meets all their assaults with a heart as firm as diamond; who conducts himself with dignity and independence; who has the bowels of a father for all his disciples; who makes no distinction between his friends and his enemies, whom he treats with equal kindness and consideration; who looks upon gold and jewels with as much indifference as if they were bits of iron and potsherds, without caring more for one than for the other; and who tries with the greatest care to remove the dense darkness of ignorance, in which the rest of mankind is plunged."

If we had not positively stated in a former part of this work (which is simply designed to give the reader some idea of the doctrines and practices of the believers in the Pitris of India) that we should refrain from the expression of any personal opinion, we might well ask ourselves whether modern Hierophants, with all their intolerance and all their pride in the morality they preach, have anything to present which will compare with the precepts here given in this, which is one of the oldest passages in the Brahminical books. Modern Gurus know full well the value of gold and precious stones, and as for the ignorance of the masses, we know what means they take to remove it.

With the aid of the Agrouchada-Parikchai, we will now take a complete survey of the higher course of philosophy pursued by the sacred decade under the direction of its Guru.

CHAPTER III.

THE GURU—EVOCATIONS.

From noon to sunset the sacred decade was under the orders of the Master of Celestial Science, or Philosophy: from sunset to midnight it passed under the direction of the Guru of Evocations, who taught the manifested part of the occult sciences.

The Book of Spirits in our possession is silent as to the formulas of evocations taught by them. According to some Brahmins, the most fearful penalties were inflicted upon the rash man who should venture to make known to a stranger the third book of the Agrouchada, treating of those matters. According to others, these formulas were never written: they were and still are verbally communicated to the adepts, in a suppressed voice.

It is also claimed, though we have had no opportunity to verify the truth of the assertion, that a peculiar language is used to express the formulas of evocation, and that it was forbidden, under penalty of death, to translate them into the vulgar tongue. The few expressions that have come to our knowledge, such as *L'rhom*, *H'hom*, *Sh'rhum*, *Sho'rhim*, are very extraordinary and do not seem to belong to any known idiom.

The Book of the Pitris gives the following portrait of the Guru of Evocations:

"The Guru of Evocations is a man who knows no other god than himself, since he has all the gods and spirits at his command." The term "gods" is here used as meaning the superior spirits. "He offers worship to Zyaus alone, the type spirit, the primordial germ, the universal womb. At his voice, rivers and seas forsake their beds, mountains become valleys and valleys become mountains. Fire, rain, and tempests are in his service. He knows the past, the present, and the future. The stars obey him, and, armed with his seven-knotted stick, he is able to confine all the evil spirits in the universe within a single magic circle." (Agrouchada-Parikchai.)

After examining the philosophical doctrines of the believers in spirits, the Pitris, we can only study the teachings of the Guru of Evocations, in the total absence of documents, as we have already taken occasion to say, in the manifestation of occult power, or exterior phenomena, produced by his disciples, the Nirvanys and Yoguys.

CHAPTER IV.

THE FRONTAL SIGN OF THE INITIATES ACCORDING TO THE AGROUCHADA-PARIKCHAI.

Every morning those who have been initiated into the third degree, after terminating their ablutions, and before going to the pagoda to listen to the discourse on the occult sciences, should trace upon their foreheads, under the direction of the Gurus, the accompanying sign, which is a symbol of the highest initiation.

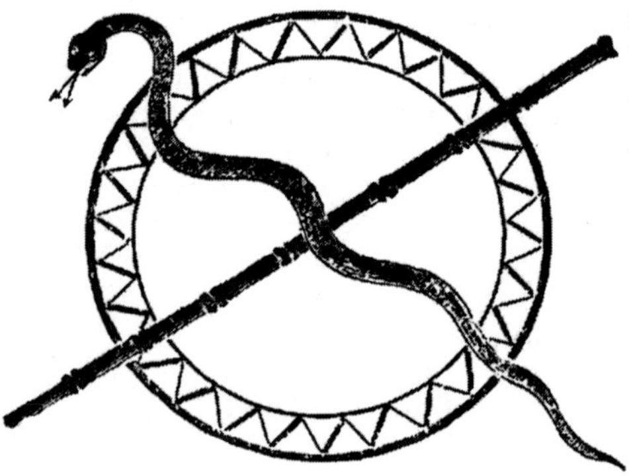

The circle indicates infinity, the study of which is the object of the occult sciences.

The border of triangles signifies that everything in nature is subject to the laws of the Trinity.

Brahma—Vischnou—Siva.
The germ—The womb—The offspring.
The seed—The earth—The plant.
The father—The mother—The child.

The serpent is a symbol of wisdom and perseverance. It also indicates that the multitude are not to be admitted to a revelation of the higher truths, which often lead weak minds to insanity and death. The seven-knotted stick represents the seven degrees of the power of evocation and external manifestation, which form the subject of study to those who have been initiated into the various degrees with which we are acquainted:

Grihasta—or House-Master.
Pourohita—or Priest of Popular Evocations.
Fakir—Performing.
Sanyassis—Superior Exorcists.
Nirvanys—Naked Evocators.
Yoguys—Contemplative.
Brahmatma—Supreme Chief.

CHAPTER V.

THE INTERPRETATION OF THE VEDAS AND OTHER WORKS OF SACRED SCRIPTURES.

Before searching the Book of the Pitris in order to see what it teaches, it may not be amiss to say a few words regarding the question of how the sacred books are to be interpreted. We deem the matter of sufficient importance to make it the subject of a separate chapter. It stands at the very threshold of our subject like a sentinel on duty.

On the first palm leaf composing the second part of the work in question we find the following words written, like an inscription, with a sharply pointed stick :

"The sacred scriptures ought not to be taken in their apparent meaning, as in the case of ordinary books. Of what use would it be to forbid their revelation to the profane if their secret meaning were contained in the literal sense of the language usually employed?

"As the soul is contained in the body,
"As the almond is hidden by its envelope,
"As the sun is veiled by the clouds,
"As the garments hide the body from view,
"As the egg is contained in its shell,
"And as the germ rests within the interior of the seed,

"So the sacred law has its body, its envelope, its cloud, its garment, its shell, which hide it from the knowledge of the world.

"All that has been, all that is, everything that will be, everything that ever has been said, are to be found in the Vedas. But the Vedas do not explain themselves, and they can only be understood when the Guru has removed the garment with which they are clothed, and scattered the clouds that veil their celestial light.

"The law is like the precious pearl that is buried in the bosom of the ocean. It is not enough to find the oyster in which it is enclosed, but it is also necessary to open the oyster and get the pearl.

"You who, in your pride, would read the sacred scriptures without the Guru's assistance, do you even know by what letter of a word you ought to begin to read them—do you know the secret of the combination by twos and threes—do you know when the final letter becomes an initial and the initial becomes final?

"Wo to him who would penetrate the real meaning of things before his head is white and he needs a cane to guide his steps."

These words of the Agrouchada, warning us against conforming to the strict letter of the sacred scriptures of India, remind us of the following words, in which Origen expresses himself like one of the initiates in the ancient temples:

"If it is incumbent upon us to adhere strictly to the letter, and to understand what is written in the law, after the manner of the Jews and of the people, I should blush to acknowledge openly that God has given us such laws—I should consider that human legislation was more elevated and rational—that of Athens, for instance, or Rome, or Lacedæmon.

"What reasonable man, I ask, would ever believe that the first, second, or third day of creation, which were divided into days and nights, could possibly exist without any sun, without any moon, and without any stars, and that during the first day there was not even any sky?

"Where shall we find any one so foolish as to believe that God actually engaged in agriculture and planted trees in the garden of Eden, which was situated in the East—that one of these trees was the tree of life and that another could impart the knowledge of good and evil? Nobody, I think, will hesitate to consider these things as figures having a mysterious meaning."

The old Jewish Cabalists, whose doctrines, as we have seen, appear to have been closely allied to those taught in the Indian temples, expressed a similar opinion in the following language:

"Wo to the man who looks upon the law as a simple record of events expressed in ordinary language, for if really that is all that it contains we can frame a law much more worthy of admiration. If we are to regard the ordinary meaning of the words we need only turn to human laws and we shall often meet with a greater degree of elevation. We have only to imitate them and to frame laws after their model and example. But it is not so: every word of the law contains a deep and sublime mystery."[1]

"The texts of the law are the garments of the law: wo to him who takes these garments for the law itself. This is the sense in which David says: 'My God, open my eyes that I may contemplate the marvels of thy law.'

"David referred to what is concealed beneath the vestments of the law. There are some foolish people who, seeing a man covered with a handsome garment, look no farther, and take the garment for the body, while there is something more precious still, and that is the soul. The law also has its body. There are the commandments which may be called the body of the law, the ordinary record of events with which it is mingled are the garments that cover the body. Ordinary people usually only regard the vestments and texts of the law; that is all they look at; they do not see what is hidden beneath the garments, but

[1] A. Franck's translation of La Kabbale.

those who are wiser pay no attention to the vestment, but to the body which is clothed by it."

"In short, the sages, the servants of the Supreme King, those who inhabit the heights of Mount Sinai, pay no regard to anything but the soul, which lies at the foundation of all the rest, which is the law itself, and in time to come they will be prepared to contemplate the soul of that soul by which the law is inspired.

"If the law were composed of words alone, such as the words of Esau, Hagar, Laban, and others, or those which were uttered by Balaam's ass or by Balaam himself, then why should it be called the law of truth, the perfect law, the faithful witness of God himself? Why should the sage esteem it as more valuable than gold or precious stones?

"But every word contains a higher meaning; every text teaches something besides the events which it seems to describe. This superior law is the more sacred, it is the real law."

It appears that the fathers of the Christian church, as well as the Jewish Cabalists and the initiates in the Hindu temples, all used the same language.

The records of the law veil its mystical meaning as the garment covers the body, as the clouds conceal the sun.

The Book of the Pitris, which we are about to examine, claims to reveal the essence, the very marrow of the vedas to those who have been initiated, but it is far from clear, except in the cosmological and philosophical portion. Whenever it treats of the rites of evocation and exorcism it resorts to obscure and mysterious formulas, to combinations of magical and occult letters, the hidden meaning of which, admitting that there is a hidden meaning, wrapped as it is in uncouth and unknown words, is quite beyond our comprehension and we have never been able to discover it.

In that portion which we propose to analyze, we shall preserve the dialogue form, as the lessons of the Guru were taught in that manner.

Apart from the belief in spirits and supernatural manifestations to which human reason does not readily assent, our readers will see that no purer morality ever grew from a more elevated system of philosophical speculation.

Upon reading these pages, they will see that antiquity has derived all the scientific knowledge of life it possessed from India, and the initiates of the Hindu temples were very much like Moses, Socrates, Plato, Aristotle, the Essenes, and the Christian apostles.

Modern spiritualism can add nothing to the metaphysical conceptions of the ancient Brahmins: that is a truth well expressed by the illustrious Cousin in the following words:

"The history of philosophy in India is an abridgement of the philosophical history of the world."

CHAPTER VI.

PSYCHOLOGY OF THE BOOK OF THE PITRIS.

The superior Guru began his lessons to those who had been admitted to the third degree of initiation, with the following aphorisms:

The first of all sciences is that of man: man is the soul; the body is only a means of communication with terrestrial matter; the study of the soul leads to the knowledge of all the visible and invisible forces of nature, to that of the Great All.

Having laid this down, the venerable priest proceeds to unveil to his audience, in the most majestic and poetic language, the mysteries of the soul. We are sorry that we are unable to accompany him as he more fully unfolds his doctrine. Our present space would not suffice. We can only give the substance of his teaching. The soul, or the ego, is a reality which manifests itself through the phenomena of which it is the cause; these phenomena are revealed to man by that interior light which the sacred books call ahancara, or conscience.

This ahancara is a universal fact and all beings are endowed with it more or less. It attains the greatest perfection in man. It is by this sovereign light, that the ego is enlightened and guided. We may say, by the way, according to the divine Manu, that from the plant, in which it seems to be in a state of suspended animation, to the animals and man, the ahancara gradually frees itself from matter by which it is encumbered, and overpowers and masters it, until it arrives at the supreme transformation, which restores the soul to liberty and enables it to continue its progressive evolution forever and ever.

Released from these ties, the soul takes no further interest in the world which it once inhabited. It continues to be an active member of the Great All, and, as says the immortal legislator:

"The ancestral spirits in an invisible state accompany the Brahmins when invited to the funeral sraddha; in an aërial form they attend them and take their place beside them, when they take their seats." (Manu, Book iii.)

As the soul approaches its last transformation, it acquires faculties of infinite perfection, and finally its only Gurus are the Pitris, or spirits who have preceded it in a higher world. By means of the pure fluid called Agasa it enters into communication with them, receives instruction from them, and, according to its deserts, acquires the power or faculty of setting in motion the secret forces of nature.

Having set this forth at length, the Guru commences his second lesson by saying that logic alone leads to a knowledge of the soul and body.

Logic is defined to be a system of laws, by the aid of which, the mind being under proper control, perfect knowledge can be attained:

First, of the soul.
Second, of the reason.
Third, of the intellect.
Seventh, of the judgment.
Eighth, of activity.
Ninth, of privation.
Tenth, of the results of actions.
Eleventh, of the faculty.
Twelfth, of suffering.
Thirteenth, of deliverance.
Fourteenth, of transmigration or metempsychosis.
Fifteenth, of the body.

Sixteenth, of the organs of sensation.

Seventeenth, of the objects of sensation.

The different modes employed by logic to arrive at a knowledge of the truth, are then studied in sixteen lessons, the headings of which are as follows:

First, evidence.

Second, the subject of study and proof, or, in other words, the cause.

Third, scientific doubt.

Fourth, motive.

Fifth, example.

Sixth, the truth demonstrated.

Seventh, the syllogism.

Eighth, demonstration per absurdum.

Ninth, the determination of the object.

Tenth, the thesis.

Eleventh, the controversy.

Twelfth, the objection.

Thirteenth, vicious arguments.

Fourteenth, perversion.

Fifteenth, of futility.

Sixteenth, of refutation.

It is unnecessary to call attention to the fact that the philosophy of Greece, as well as of modern Europe, seems to be largely indebted to that of the Hindus.

We shall not dwell further upon these various points. The enumeration is alone sufficient to show how much further they might be developed. Suffice it to say, that they are treated in a most masterly manner by the old philosophers on the banks of the Ganges, whose whole life was spent in study of the most elevated speculations.

Proof in general is made in four ways:

First, by perception,

Second, by induction.

Third, by comparison.

Fourth, by testimony.

Induction, in its turn, is divided:

First, into antecedent, which separates the effect from the cause.

Second, into consequent, which deduces the cause from the effect.

Third, into analogy, which infers that unknown things are alike from known things that are alike.

After analyzing the soul and body, and testing them in all their manifestations in the crucible of logic, the Book of the Pitris, through the mouth of the Guru, gives the following list of their faculties and qualities:

Faculties of the Soul.

First, sensibility.
Second, intelligence.
Third, will.

Faculties of the Intellect.

First, conscience, or organs of internal perception.
Second, sense, or organs of external perception.
Third, memory.
Fourth, imagination.
Fifth, reason, or organs of absolute notions, or axioms.

Qualities of the Body.

First, color (sight).
Second, savor (taste).
Third, odor (smell).
Fourth, the sense of hearing and touch.
Fifth, number.
Sixth, quantity.
Seventh, individuality.
Eighth, conjunction.
Ninth, disjunction.
Tenth, priority.

Eleventh, posteriority.
Twelfth, gravity, or weight.
Thirteenth, fluidity.
Fourteenth, viscidity.
Fifteenth, sound.

As there is nothing material about anything that proceeds from the soul, it is obvious that those faculties which emanate from the *Ahancara*, or inward light, and the *Agasa* or pure fluid, cannot under any circumstances and however thoroughly we may study them, be made the objects of sensation, and it follows that the final end of all science is to free the spirit at the earliest possible moment from all material fetters, from the bonds of passion, and any evil influences that stand in the way of its passage to the celestial spheres, which are inhabited by aërial beings whose transmigrations are ended.

The body, on the contrary, being solely composed of material molecules, is dissolved into its original elements, and returns to the earth from which it sprung.

If the soul, however, is not deemed worthy to receive the fluidic body, spoken of by Manu, it is compelled to commence a new series of transmigrations in this world, until it has attained the requisite degree of perfection, when it abandons the human form forever.

It is impossible to shut our eyes to the extraordinary similarity between this system of philosophy and that of the old Greek philosophers, and especially of Pythagoras, who believed in the doctrine of metempsychosis, and also held that the object of all philosophy was to free the soul from its mortal envelope and guide it to the world of spirits. Although it appears from all the traditions relating to the subject, that Pythagoras went to the Indus in Alexander's train and travelled in India and brought back this system from there, and was the only one of all the old Sophists that taught it, some people who have no eyes for anything that is not Greek, would have us believe that India was indebted to the land of Socrates for its earliest knowledge of philosophy. We will merely repeat, in reply, the words of the illustrious Colebrook, who has studied this question for thirty years in India on the spot:

"In philosophy the Hindus are the masters of the Greeks, and not their disciples."

Pythagoras believed in a hierarchy of the superior spirits, exercising various degrees of influence upon worldly matters. That doctrine lies at the very foundation of the occult sciences. It necessarily supposes an acquaintance with the magical formulas of evocation, and while the philosopher only leads us to suppose that he had been admitted to a knowledge of supernatural sciences, there is reason to believe that in this he was deterred from telling all he knew by the terrible oath taken by all those who had been initiated.

The Guru ended his inquiries into the soul and its faculties by the study of the reason.

As the whole logical power of Hindu spiritism rests upon these faculties, we devote a special chapter to the superior Guru's discourse upon this interesting subject. We will give the introduction merely in the form of a dialogue.

We use the modern term spiritism, to designate the Hindu belief in the Pitris, for the reason that no other word exists in our language which sufficiently characterizes it.

The belief in the Pitris is a positive belief in spirits as manifesting themselves to and directing men: it matters little whether the word has any scientific value or not. It is enough that it correctly expresses the idea which we wish to convey.

CHAPTER VII.

REASON.

[From the twenty-third dialogue of the Second Book of the Agrouchada-Parikchai.]

VATU [1] (the Disciple).

Our ablutions have been performed, as prescribed. The regular sacrifices have all been accomplished, the fire slumbers upon the hearthstone. The pestle no longer resounds in the mortar as the young women prepare their evening food. The sacred elephants have just struck upon copper gongs the strokes that divide the night. It is now midnight. It is the hour when you commence your sublime lessons.

THE GURU.

My children, what would you of me?

VATU.

O thou, who art adorned with every virtue, who art as great as Mount Hymavat (Himalaya), who art possessed of a perfect knowledge of the four Vedas and of everything that is explained in the sacred word, thou who possessest all the mentrams (or formulas of evocation), who holdest the superior shades and spirits suspended

---

[1] This word in Sanscrit signifies novice or pupil; it is applied to any one, no matter what his age may be, who studies under the direction of a Guru.

from thy lips, whose shining virtues are as brilliant as the sun, whose reputation is everywhere known, and who art praised in the fourteen heavens by the fourteen classes of spirits who communicate with men, let thy science flow over us, who embrace thy sacred feet, as the waters of the Ganges flow over the plains they fertilize.

THE GURU.

Listen while the vile Soudra sleeps like a dog beneath the poyal of his abode: while the Vaysia is dreaming of the hoards of this world's treasures that he is accumulating, and while the Xchatria, or king, sleeps among his women, faint with pleasure but never satiated, this is the moment when just men, who are not under the dominion of their flesh, commence the study of the sciences.

THE VATU.

Master, we are listening.

THE GURU.

Age has weakened my sight, and this feeble body is hardly able to unfold to you what I mean: my envelope is falling asunder and the hour of my transfiguration is approaching. What did I promise you for this evening?

THE VATU.

Master, you said to us, I will unfold to you the knowledge of the immortal light, which puts man in communication with infinity and rules his transformations upon earth.

THE GURU.

You will now hear a voice and that voice will be mine, but the thought that arises in my mind is not mine. Listen: I give place to the superior spirits by whom I am inspired.

The Guru then performs an evocation to the marîtchis, or primordial spirits. The following is a brief summary of his discourse.

Every man is conscious within himself of certain absolute notions, existing outside of matter and sensation, which he has not derived from education and which his reason has received from Swayambhouva, or the Self-existent Being, as a sign of his immortal origin.

They are the principles:

Of cause.

Of identity.

Of contradiction.

Of harmony.

Through the principle of cause reason tells us that everything that exists is the result of some cause or other, and though the latter often escapes our notice, we still acknowledge its existence, knowing it to be a fact.

This is the source of all science: we study realities only to trace them back to their producer.

It is not enough to lay down the law of a fact. We must know whom the law proceeds from, and what maintains the harmony of nature.

Through the principles of identity and contradiction, man knows that his ego is not that of his neighbor. That two contrary facts are not governed by the same law; that good is not evil; that two contraries cannot simultaneously be predicated of the same fact.

Through the principle of harmony, reason tells us that everything in the universe is subject to certain immutable laws, and the principle of cause compels us to attribute to these laws an author and preserver.

No faculty of the soul is able to perform any act or motion, except in conformity with these principles, which regulate its interior and exterior life, its spiritual and material nature. Without these principles, to which all are necessarily obliged to submit, and which commend themselves to the reason of all men and people, without these principles, we say, which are the supreme law of all observation, of all investigation, of all science, no one can derive any benefit from tradition, or from the achievements of those who have preceded him. There being no other axiomatic foundation for scientific facts, there can be no science, for no two men will see, think, or judge alike.

Human reason, universal reason, guided by absolute principles—that is the bright light, guiding and uniting all men in a common work for the benefit of all.

Such is a brief abstract of this dialogue, which covers fifty palm-leaves at least of the Book of the Pitris.

It would be impossible for us, as may well be imagined, in the present work, which is merely a brief history or description of the practices of those who have been initiated, and in which, in order to accomplish the task we have set before us, we are obliged to compress the substance of more than fifty volumes, to give any subject a disproportionate or undue importance.

With the help of the axioms laid down by the Guru, reason leads man to the knowledge:

First, of the Supreme Being.

Second, of the constitution of the universe.

Third, of superior and inferior spirits.

Fourth, of man.

We propose now to show what is the belief of those who have been initiated upon each of these matters.

CHAPTER VIII.

A TEXT FROM THE VEDAS.

Nothing is commenced or ended. Everything is changed or transformed. Life and death are only modes of transformation which rule the vital molecule, from the plant up to Brahma himself. (Atharva-Veda.)

CHAPTER IX.

A FEW SLOCAS FROM MANU.

The soul is the assemblage of the gods. The universe rests in the supreme soul. It is the soul that accomplishes the series of acts emanating from animate beings.

*
* *

The Brahmin should figure to himself the great being which is the Sovereign Master of the universe, and who is subtler than an atom, as more brilliant than pure gold, and as inconceivable by the mind, except in the repose of the most abstract contemplation.

*
* *

Some worship him in the fire, some in the air; he is the Lord of creation, the eternal Brahma.

*
* *

He it is who, enveloping all beings in a body composed of the five elements, causes them to pass through the successive stages of birth, growth, and dissolution, with a movement like that of a wheel.

*
* *

So the man who recognizes the supreme soul as present in his own soul, understands that it is his duty to be kind and true to all, and the most fortunate destiny that he could have desired is that of being finally absorbed in Brahma. (Manu, Book xii.)

CHAPTER X.

OF THE SUPREME BEING.

[Twenty-fourth dialogue of the Book of the Pitris.]

After giving as a text the words of the Atharva-Veda, and a few verses from Manu, which we have just quoted, the Agrouchada-Parikchai devotes the twenty-fourth lesson of the Guru to the study of the Supreme Being. The principles of cause and harmony lead human reason to the absolute notion of a *superior and universal cause.*

"He who denies this cause for the whole," says the Book of the Pitris, "has no right to assign any cause to any particular fact. If you say the universe exists because it exists, it is unnecessary to go any further; man lives only by facts, and he has no assurance otherwise of the invariability of natural laws."

Having shown that the belief in a superior and universal cause, in the Supreme Being, lies at the basis of all science and, pre-eminently, of axiomatic truth, the Guru of initiations borrows from Manu and the Vedas the definition of this primordial force, whose mysterious and sacred name it is forbidden to utter.

"It is he who exists by himself, and who is in all, because all is in him.

"It is he who exists by himself, because the mind alone can perceive him; who cannot be apprehended by our sensual organs. Who is without visible parts, eternal the soul of all beings, and none can comprehend him.

"He is one, immutable, devoid of parts or form, infinite, omniscient, omnipresent, and omnipotent. He it is who has created the heavens and the worlds out of chaos, and has set them whirling through infinite space. He is the motor, the great original substance, the efficient and material cause of everything."

"Behold the Ganges as it rolls, it is he; the ocean as it mutters, it is he; the cloud as it thunders, it is he; the lightning as it flashes, it is he; as from all eternity the world was in the mind of Brahma, so now everything that exists is in his image."

"He is the author and principle of all things, eternal, immaterial, everywhere present, independent, infinitely happy, exempt from all pain or care, the pure truth, the source of all justice, he who governs all, who disposes of all, who rules all, infinitely enlightened, infinitely wise, without form, without features, without extent, without condition, without name, without caste, without relation, of a purity that excludes all passion, all inclination, all compromise."

The Guru, with the Pouranas, discusses these sublime questions, to which he returns the following answers:

"Mysterious spirit, immense force, inscrutable power, how was thy power, thy force, thy life manifested before the period of creation? Wast thou dormant in the midst of disintegrating matter, like an extinct sun? Was the dissolution of matter in thyself or was it by thy order? Wert thou chaos? Did thy life include all the lives that had escaped the shock of the destroying elements? If thou wert life, thou wert also death, for there can be no destruction without movement, and motion could not exist without thee."

"Didst thou cast the worlds into a blazing furnace in order that they might be regenerated, in order that they might be born again, from their decomposing elements, as an old tree springs again from the seed in the midst of its corruption?"

"Did thy spirit wander over the waters, thy name being Narayana?

"The immortal germ," went on the Guru, "whose terrible name should not be spoken, is the ancient of days. Nothing existed without him; nothing was apart from him; he causeth life, motion, and light to shine through infinity; everything comes from him and everything goes back to him; he is constantly fertilizing the universe, through an intimate union with his productive thought.

"Hear ye, this has been revealed to the sages in the silence of solitary places, upon the banks of unfrequented torrents, in the mysterious crypts of temples."

* * *

This is what no profane ear should hear. This is what has been from all eternity, which never had any beginning and will have no end.

* * *

Listen to the hymn of eternal love:

* * *

He is one and he is two. He is two, but he is three. The one contains two principles, and the union of these two principles produces the third.

* * *

He is one and he is all, and this one contains the husband and the wife, and the love of the husband for the wife, and of the wife for the husband, produces the third, which is the son.

* * *

The husband is as ancient as the wife, and the wife is as ancient as the husband, and the son is also as ancient as the husband and wife, and the one that contains all three is called

A
U M

Three in One.

This is given as the meaning of the sublime monosyllable. It is the image of the ancient of days.

* * *

The union of the husband and the wife continues forever, and from the transports of their eternal love the son constantly receives life, which he unceasingly drops into infinity, like so many millions of dew-drops fertilized by the divine love.

* * *

Every drop of dew that falls is an exact representation of the great all, an atom of the Paramatma or universal soul, and each of these atoms possesses the two principles that beget the third.

* * *

So everything goes by three in the universe, from the infinite to which everything descends, to the infinite to which everything ascends, with a motion similar to that of an endless chain revolving about a wheel.

* * *

The first appearance of atoms is in the state of fertilized germs. They collect together and form matter which is being continually transformed and improved by the three grand principles of life; water, and heat, and by the pure fluid, called Agasa.

* * *

Agasa, the pure fluid, is life itself. It is the soul. It is man. The body is only an envelope, an obedient slave.

As the seed, which germinates, bursts through its shell, and shoots out of the ground, Agasa lays gradually aside the material veil, beneath which its transformation takes place, and purifies itself. Upon leaving the earth, it passes through the fourteen more perfect regions, and every time it abandons its former envelope, and clothes itself with one more pure.

* * *

Agasa, the vital fluid—the soul—animates the human body upon earth. In infinite space, it put on the aërial form of the Pitris or spirits.

* * *

Human souls before being absorbed in the supreme soul, ascend through the fourteen following degrees of superior spirits.

The Pitris are the immediate souls of our ancestors, still living in the terrestrial circle, and communicating with men, just as more perfect man communicates with the animal world.

* * *

Above the Pitris, but having nothing in common with the earth, are,

The somapas, The agnidagdhas, The agnanidagdhas, The agnichwattas, The cavias, The barhichads, The sômyas, The havichmats, The adjyapas, The soucalis, The sadhyas.	Spirits inhabiting the planets and stars.

The two highest degrees were those of the Marîtchis and of the Pradjapatis, who were superior spirits, and would soon arrive at the end of their transmigrations and be absorbed in the great soul.

* * *

This is called the progressive transformation of just spirits who have spent their terrestrial life in the practice of virtue. The following are the transformations of the bad spirits:

The yakchas, The rakchasas, The pisatchas, The gandharbas, The apsaras, The assouras, The nagas, The sarpas, The souparnas, The kinnaras.	Bad spirits who are constantly attempting to creep into the bodies of men, and return to terrestrial life, which they have to pass through anew.

* * *

These bad spirits are the malign secretions of the universe. Their only means of regaining the degree of purity required for the higher transformations, is through thousands and thousands of transformations into minerals, plants, and animals.

The superior pradjapatis are ten in number; the three first,

Marîtchi,
Atri,
Angiras,

represent eternal reason, wisdom, and intelligence.

The second three,

Poulastya,
Poulaha,
Cratou,

represent the goodness, power, and majesty of the Divine Being.

* * *

The last triad,

Vasichta,
Pratchetas,
Brighou,

are the agents of creation, preservation, and transformation. They are the direct ministers of the manifested trinity.

* * *

The last, called

Narada,

represents the intimate union of all the Pradjapatis in the mind of the Self-existent Being, and the unceasing production of the thousands of beings by whom nature is constantly being rejuvenated and the work of creation is being perpetuated.

* * *

These qualities of reason, wisdom, intelligence, goodness, power, majesty, creation, preservation, transformation, and union, which are being constantly diffused throughout nature, under the influence of the superior spirits, are the unceasing product of the love of the divine husband for his celestial spouse. In this way the great being maintains his eternal life, which is that of all beings.

* * *

For all things in the universe only exist and move and undergo transformation, in order that the existence of the Great All may be perpetuated, renewed, and purified.

That is the reason why nothing exists outside of his essence and substance, and that all creatures contain in themselves the principles of reason, wisdom, intelligence, goodness, power, majesty, creation, preservation, transformation, and union, and are the image of the ten Pradjapatis, who are themselves a direct emanation from the divine power.

* * *

The departure of the soul-atom from the bosom of divinity is a radiation from the life of the *Great All*, who expends his strength in order that he may grow again, and in order that he may live by its return. God thereby acquires a new vital force, purified by all the transformations that the soul-atom has undergone.

* * *

Its return is the final reward. Such is the secret of the evolutions of the Great Being, and of the supreme soul, the mother of all souls.

After fully setting forth the above system with regard to God, the soul, and perpetual creation, the most astonishing system, perhaps, that the world has ever produced, and which contains within itself, substantially under a mystical form, all the philosophical doctrines that have ever agitated the human mind, the Book of the Pitris closes the present chapter, from which we have eliminated its interminable invocations and hymns to the creative power, by the following comparison :

"The Great All, which is constantly in motion and is constantly undergoing change in the visible and invisible universe, is like the tree which perpetuates itself by its seed, and is unceasingly creating the same identical types."

Thus, according to the belief of those who had been initiated, God is the whole, the soul is the atom which undergoes progressive transformation, is purified and ascends to its eternal source, and the universe is the reunited body of atoms in process of transformation.

As man upon earth is in direct communication with the souls of plants and of inferior animals, so the Pitris, having clothed themselves with a fluidic (fluidique) body, and having attained the first of the fourteen superior degrees, are always in communication with man.

There is an uninterruptedly ascending scale, the links of which are never broken :

The Pitris are in relation with the Somapas (spirits).

The Somapas with the Agnidagdhas.

The Agnidagdhas with the Agnanidagdhas.

The Agnanidagdhas with the Agnichwatas.

And so on up to the Pradjapatis, who are in direct communication with God.

In each of these categories the spirit assumes a more perfect body and continues to move in a circle of laws, which may be called *superterrestrial* but which are not *supernatural.*

The Book of the Pitris says positively that the spirits preserve their sex, whatever may be the superior categories to which they may attain ; that they are united together by the ties of a love which is totally unlike every form of earthly passion. These unions are always prolific and give birth to beings who possess all the qualities of their parents, enjoy the same happiness, and are not tied down to the transformations of this lower world.

It is possible, however, as the Pitris enjoy the utmost freedom of will, that they may commit some exceptionally grave fault and be degraded, in consequence, to the condition of man. Upon this point the Agrouchada-Parikchai alludes to a revolt of the Pitris, that happened a long while ago, but makes no further explanation. Some of them are supposed to have been cast down to earth again.

There is every reason to suppose, from the close similarity existing between their various religious traditions, that this legend found its way, through the process of initiation, from the Hindu temples into the mysteries of Chaldea and Egypt, and thus gave birth to the myth of the first sin.

Those Pitris which have not passed the degree immediately above that of man, are the only spirits which are in communication with the latter. They are regarded as the ancestors of the human race and its natural directors from whom it derives its inspiration. They are themselves inspired by the spirits of the next degree above them, and so on, from one degree to another, until the divine word or, in other terms, until revelation is imparted to man.

The Pitris are not equal to each other. Each category forms a separate and complete world, in the likeness of our own, only more perfect, in which there is the same diversity of intelligence and function.

According to this theory, it will be readily understood that man cannot live isolated from his ancestors. It is only by the aid of their instruction and help that he can arrive in the shortest possible time at the transformation by means of which he becomes united to them.

Upon this belief is based the whole theory of initiation.

But men upon earth are not fitted to receive communications from a higher world. Some are naturally inclined toward evil and do not care to improve their characters: others still feel the effect of the previous lives which they have spent in the form of animals, and their spirits are entirely dominated by matter. It is only after many generations have been spent in the practice of virtue that the soul becomes spiritualized and the pure fluid called Agasa is developed, by means of which communication is established.

Hence the natural inequality of men and the necessity that those who have arrived at the highest degree of development should unite in the study of the great secrets of life and of the forces of nature, that they may set them in motion.

"It is only by constant fasting, mortification, prayer, and meditation," says the Agrouchada-Parikchai, "that man can arrive at complete separation from everything that surrounds him. In that case he acquires extraordinary power. Time, space, capacity, weight are of no consequence. He has all the Pitris at his command and through them all the superior spirits likewise. He attains a power of thought and action of which formerly he had no conception, and sees through the curtain that hangs before the splendors of human destiny."

But while there are mediating and directing spirits who are always ready to come at his call, to point the way to virtue, there are also others which have been condemned for their misdeeds in this, their earthly life, to undergo again all their previous transmigrations, commencing with mineral and plant life; they float about in infinity until they can seize upon some unoccupied particle of matter, which they can use as an envelope: they employ all the resources of their miserable intellects to deceive and mislead men as to the means by which they can arrive at the supreme and final transformation. These bad spirits are constantly occupied in tormenting pious hermits during their sacrifices, initiates in the midst of their studies, and sannyassis in their prayers, and it is impossible to drive them away, except through the possession of the secret of magical conjurations.

Lastly, the whole system, the Great All, is perpetually preserved, developed, and transformed through love.

The emblem of this love, the Trinity, contains within itself both the husband and wife, and their perpetual embraces give birth to the son by whom the universe is regenerated. Everything that exists is composed of atoms that reproduce themselves by threes—the germ, the womb, and the offspring—the father, the mother, the child—after the pattern of that immortal Trinity which is welded together in one being by whom the whole of nature is ruled, and the soul-atom, at the close of its transformations, returns to the ever-living source from which it sprang.

This grand and imposing conception gave birth, in the vulgar cult, to that triple manifestation of the Trinity which was known in India as—

Nara—Agni—Brahma—the Father,
Nari—Vaya—Vischnou—the Mother,
Viradj—Sourya—Siva—the Son.

It was known in Egypt under the following names:

Amon—Osiris—Horus—the Father,
Mouth—Isis—Isis—the Mother,
Khons—Horus—Malouli—the Son.

It was called in Chaldea:

Anou,
Nouah,
Bel.

In Polynesian Oceanica:

Taaroa,
Ina,
Oro.

And finally in Christianity:

The Father,
The Spirit,
The Word.

All the teachings of the temples grow out of the mysteries into which the priests are initiated, and which they change into the grossest symbols, in order to vulgarize them without divulging their secret meaning.

CHAPTER XI.

WORDS SPOKEN BY THE PRIESTS AT MEMPHIS.

The vandalism committed by Cæsar's soldiers in the destruction of the Alexandrian library has left us nothing but sculptures and inscriptions with which to reconstruct the religious history of Egypt. But that country was so directly allied to India that its ruins speak to us in a voice full of meaning, and its inscriptions are pregnant with significance, when studied from a Brahminical point of view.

We will merely mention, at present, one inscription taken from the Rahmesséum at Thebes, which is a complete summary of the doctrine of the Pitris, as herein set forth.

One of the first expressions that the Egyptian priests made use of in addressing those who had been passed through the process of initiation was as follows:

Everything is contained and preserved in one,
Everything is changed and transformed by three,
The Monad created the Dyad,
The Dyad begat the Triad,
The Triad shines throughout the whole of nature.

CHAPTER XII.

THE FORMULAS OF EVOCATION.

After an examination of the part performed by the human soul, and the superior and inferior spirits, as well as by the universe, in the Great All which we call God, and, having established the ties of relationship existing between all souls, in consequence of which, those belonging to the superior groups are always ready to aid souls belonging to an inferior group with their counsel and communications, the Book of the Pitris goes on to discuss the mysterious subject of evocations. Evocations are of two sorts.

They are addressed either to disembodied spirits or to ancestral spirits, in which latter case the spirits evoked can respond to the appeal made to them, whatever may be the superior degree to which they may have attained, or they are addressed to spirits not included in the genealogical line of relationship, and then the evocations are unsuccessful if addressed to spirits who have already passed the degree immediately above that of man.

The following rules may be laid down:

That a man can evoke the spirit of his ancestor under any circumstances, even if the latter has already arrived at the rank of Pradjapati, or supreme director of creation, and is on the point of being absorbed in the Great Soul.

That if any one evokes a spirit not in his genealogical line, he can only obtain manifestations from those who belong to the class of Pitris.

Preparations should be made for the ceremony of evocation by fasting and prayer, for, as the Agrouchada-Parikchai says, these terrible formulas are fatal when not uttered by a pure mouth. In order to evoke a spirit the priest should:

First, isolate himself entirely from all external matters.

Second, his mind should be absorbed in thought of the spirit whose appearance he has called forth and from whom he desires to receive a communication.

Third, he should enclose all the malign spirits who might disturb him in a magic circle.

Fourth, he should offer up sacrifices to his ancestral shades and to the superior spirits.

Fifth, he should pronounce the formulas of evocation.

A special part of the Book of the Pitris is devoted to these formulas, which all have a cabalistic meaning. We shall make no effort to elucidate this point any further, as we were never able to obtain the key to these various combinations from the Brahmins. We should be careful to avoid attaching greater importance to these matters than they are fairly entitled to.

The first leaf of the chapter on formulas contains the following epigraph, the combinations of words and letters being as simple as they could well be. We give it as a specimen to show what puerile methods the priests resorted to in order to cover up their practices.

As it contains no formula of evocation, the Brahmins had no objection to explain its meaning:

Nid + Nad
Irt
Mad + uo—yâç—ad
Irt
mav—id
Irt
sam + ad
Irt
mal + ak
Irt
Mam + ra + dî—yart
Tag—aj
Irt.

By reading from right to left, commencing with the last syllable of each word, we are able to attach the following meaning to this cabalistic sentence:

Tridandin.
Tridaçâyoudam.
Tridivam.
Tridamas.
Trikalam.
Trayîdarmam.
Trijagat.

* * *

The language of evocations totally dispenses with all verbs, prepositions, conjunctions, and adverbs, and while names are retained, they undergo the terminations of the different declensions by which the grammatic action of the verbs and prepositions understood, is indicated.

Thus, in the case under consideration:

Tridandin is in the nominative, and signifies the priest who is entitled to three sticks. These three sticks indicate one who has been admitted to the third degree of initiation, and who has power over three things: thought, speech, and action.

Tridaçâyoudam signifies the divine arm. This word is in the accusative, and is governed by a verb of which Tridandin is the subject.

Tridivam signifies the triple heaven. This word is also in the accusative and is consequently in the same situation as the preceding word.

Tridamas is the name of Agni of three fires. This word is the genitive of a word of which Tridamam is the nominative.

Trikalam signifies the three times, the past, the present, the future. This is also in the accusative form.

Trayîdarmam is in the accusative, and signifies the three books of the law.

Trijagat is in the neutral form of the accusative and signifies the three worlds: heaven, earth, and the lower regions.

According to the Brahmins, this inscription means as follows:

Tridandin—or he who has been initiated into three degrees, who carries the three rods, and who has power over three things: thought, speech, and action.

Tridaçâyoudam—if he desires to secure possession of the divine arm.

Tridivam—and conquer the power of evocation from the spirit of the three heavens.

Tridamas—must have in his service Agni of the three fires.

Trikalam—and know the three times, past, present, and future.

Trayîdarmam—must possess the essence of the three books of the law.

Trijagat—thus he will be enabled to know the secrets of the three worlds.

We do not propose to dwell at length upon the practice of occult writing, the mechanism of which changes with every form of evocation. Besides, it has been impossible for us, as we have elsewhere stated, to obtain possession of that part of the Book of the Pitris containing these formulas. The priests keep them to themselves and the people are not allowed to know anything about them.

At one time the penalty for divulging a single verse of the Book of Spirits was death. The rank of the accused made no difference. It mattered not that the guilty priest belonged to the sacerdotal caste.

Neither did the Jewish Cabalists limit themselves to the symbolical language with which they covered up their doctrines. They also endeavored to introduce into their writings secret methods almost identical with those of the Indian pagodas.

As for particular ceremonies of evocation, we shall have occasion to study them in all their details when we turn our attention to the external manifestations produced by the different grades of initiates.

CHAPTER XIII.

FORMULAS OF MAGICAL INCANTATION—VULGAR MAGIC.

The formulas of magical incantation, addressed to evil spirits, are kept as secret as those used in the evocation of superior spirits. They even form a part of a special book of the Agrouchada called the Agrouchada-Parikchai, treating of magicians.

They are also written, as well as read, in a manner similar to that we have just described, in order to hide from the profane their real meaning. We pass them over, however, and turn our attention to the external manifestations, exorcisms, and cases of demoniacal possession which are so frequent in India.

We propose to give an impartial account of the numerous facts that have fallen under our own observation, some of which are so extraordinary from a physiological, as well as from a purely spiritual point of view, that we hardly know what to say of them.

We merely allude to the chapter of the Agrouchada treating of formulas of incantation and are unable to give any further information as to the magical words, to which the priests attribute so much virtue in exorcising Rakchasas, Pisatchas, Nagas, Souparnas, and other evil spirits that frequent funeral ceremonies, take possession of men's bodies, and disturb the sacrifices.

We have already, in another work,[1] discussed that portion of the Book of the Pitris, notwithstanding its vul-

---

[1] History of the Virgins.

garity, and we see no reason to change the opinion therein expressed, which it may not be amiss to call to the reader's mind. He will excuse us for quoting ourselves :

Magic seems to have established itself in India, as in some highly favored spot. In that country nothing is attributed to ordinary causes, and there is no act of malignancy or of wickedness of which the Hindus deem their magicians incapable.

Disappointments, obstacles, accidents, diseases, untimely deaths, the barrenness of women, miscarriages, epizootics, in short, all the ills that humanity is heir to, are attributed to the occult and diabolical practices of some wicked magician, in the pay of an enemy.

If an Indian, when he meets with a misfortune, happens to be on bad terms with anybody, his suspicions are immediately directed in that quarter, and he accuses his enemy of resorting to magic in order to injure him.

The latter, however, resents the imputation. Their feelings become embittered against each other, the disagreement soon extends to their relatives and friends, and the consequences often become serious.

As malign spirits are exorcised, pursued, and hunted by the followers of the Pitris, it is the vulgar belief that they enter the service of vagabonds and miscreants, and teach them special magical formulas, by which they seek together to do all possible harm to others.

Several thousand years of sacerdotal despotism, during which every means have been employed to keep the people in ignorance and superstition, have carried popular credulity to its highest pitch.

In the South of India particularly we constantly meet with crowds of soothsayers and sorcerers, vending their oracles to any one who would purchase them, and spreading before rich and poor alike for a consideration the pretended mystery of human destiny.

These people are not much dreaded.

But there are others, whose diabolical art is thought to be unlimited, and who are supposed to possess all the secrets of magic.

To inspire love or hatred, to introduce the devil into any one's body, or to drive him away, to cause sudden death or an incurable disease, to produce contagious maladies in cattle, or to protect them therefrom, to discover the most secret things, and to find lost or stolen articles—all this is but child's play for them.

The mere sight of one who is supposed to be endowed with such vast power inspires the Hindu with the deepest terror.

These doctors of magic are often consulted by persons who have enemies, of whom they desire to be revenged, by means of sorcery. On the other hand, when any one who suffers from disease attributes it to a cause of this kind, he calls in their aid, that they may deliver him by a counter-charm, or transfer the disease to those who have so maliciously caused it in his case.

The supplementary volume of the Agrouchada-Parikchai, treating of the practices of vulgar magic, does not seem to question them in any respect; it merely attributes them to the influence of evil spirits.

In its view, the magician's power is immense, but he only uses it for evil purposes.

Nothing is easier than for him to afflict any one whom he may meet with fever, dropsy, epilepsy, insanity, a constant nervous trembling, or any other disease, in short. But that is nothing. By his art he can even cause the entire destruction of an army besieging a city, or the sudden death of the commander of a besieged city and of all its inhabitants.

But while magic teaches how to do harm, it also shows us how to prevent it. There is no magician so shrewd that there is not another who can more than match him in ability, or destroy the effect of his charms, and make them rebound upon himself or his patrons.

Independent of their direct intervention, the magicians have a large assortment of amulets, talismans, and powerful and efficient preservatives against sorcery and enchantments, in which they do a large business and make a great deal of money.

They consist of glass beads, enchanted by mentrams, of dried and aromatic roots and herbs, of sheets of copper upon which cabalistic characters, uncouth figures, and fantastical words are engraved.

The Hindus of the lower castes always wear them upon their persons, thinking that a supply of these relics will protect them from all harm.

Secret preparations to inspire love, to kindle anew an expiring passion, to restore vigor to the weak and infirm, come also within the province of the magicians, and are by no means the least unproductive source of their income.

It is to them a woman always applies first when she wishes to reclaim a faithless husband, or prevent his becoming such.

It is by the aid of the philters they concoct that a young libertine or a sweetheart usually tries to beguile or captivate the object of his passion.

The Agrouchada also discusses the subject of incubi. "These demons in India," says Dubois, "are much worse and more diabolical, than those spoken of by Delrio the Jesuit, in his 'Disquisitiones Magicæ.' By their violent and long-continued embraces they so weary the women whom they visit in the form of a dog, a tiger, or some other animal, that the poor creatures often die of fatigue and exhaustion."

It then speaks at some length of the means by which weapons may be enchanted or bewitched.

These arms upon which magical mentrams have been pronounced, have the virtue of producing effects which will compare in every respect with those caused by the celebrated sword of Durandal, or the lance of Argail, by which so many were disabled.

The Hindu gods and giants, in their frequent wars with each other, always made use of enchanted arms.

Nothing could withstand, for instance, the arrow of Brahma, which was never unsheathed without destroying an entire army; or the arrow of the serpent Capel, which, whenever it was cast among his enemies, had the property of throwing them into a state of lethargy which, as may well be imagined, put them at a great disadvantage and contributed largely to their defeat.

There is no secret that magic does not teach. There are magical secrets how to acquire wealth and honors; to render sterile women prolific by rubbing the hands and feet with certain enchanted compounds; to discover treasures buried in the earth, or concealed in some secret place, no matter where; and to make the bearer invulnerable, or even invincible, in battle.

The only thing they are not so clear about is the subject of everlasting life; and yet who can tell how many alchemists have grown white in the crypts of the pagodas, and how many strange philters have been there concocted in order to learn the secret of immortality?

To become expert in magic the pupil must learn from a magician himself, whom the sorcerers call their Guru, like the believers in the philosophical doctrine of the Pitris, the formulas of evocation, by means of which the malign spirits are brought into complete subjection.

Some of these spirits the magician evokes in preference to others, probably on account of their willingness to do anything that may be required of them.

In the first rank are the spirits of certain planets. The name, Grahas, which is used to designate them, means the act of seizing or taking possession of those whom they are commanded, by a magical incantation, to torment.

In the next rank come the boutams, or demons from

the lower regions, representing each a principle of destruction, the pisatchas, rakchasas, nagas, and other evil spirits.

The chaktys are female genii, who force men whom they meet at night.

The malign spirits are Kali, the Goddess of Blood, Marana-Devy, the Goddess of Death, and the others whom we have enumerated.

In order to set them in motion the magician has recourse to various mysterious operations, such as mentrams, sacrifices, and other different formulas. He should be nude when he addresses himself to goddesses, and modestly clothed when he addresses himself to male spirits.

The flowers that he offers to the spirits evoked by him should all be red, and the boiled rice should be colored with the blood of a young virgin, or a child, in case he proposes to cause death.

The mentrams, or prayers, which have such efficacy in all magical matters, exercise such an ascendancy upon the superior spirits themselves that the latter are powerless to refuse to do whatever the magician may order, in heaven, in the air, or upon the earth.

But those which are most certain and irresistible in their effects are what are called the fundamental mentrams, and consist of various fantastical monosyllables, of uncouth sound and difficult pronunciation, after the manner of those which we have already given while speaking of the formulas used by the priests.

Sometimes the magician repeats his mentrams in a respectful tone, ending all his evocations with the word *Namaha*, meaning respectful greeting, and loading the spirit that he has evoked with praises. At other times he speaks to them in an imperious and dictatorial tone, exclaiming in angry accents:

"If you are willing to do what I ask you, that is enough; if not, I command you in the name of such and such a god."

Thereupon the spirit had to submit.

It would be impossible to enumerate the different drugs, ingredients, and implements that compose the stock-in-trade of a magician.

There are some spells in which it is necessary to use the bones of sixty-four different kinds of animals, neither more nor less, and among them are included those of a man born on the first day of the new moon, or of a woman, or a virgin, or a child, or a pariah.

When all these bones, being mingled together, are enchanted by mentrams and consecrated by sacrifices, and are buried in an enemy's house or at his door, upon a night ascertained to be propitious, after an inspection of the stars for that purpose, his death will infallibly follow.

In like manner, if the magician, in the silence of night, should bury the bones in question in an enemy's camp at the four cardinal points of the compass, and then, retiring to a distance, should pronounce the mentram of defeat, all the troops there encamped would utterly perish, or else would scatter to the four winds of heaven, of their own accord, before seven days had elapsed.

Thirty-two enchanted arms thrown among a besieging army would cause such a fright that a hundred men would seem like a thousand.

Of a mixture of earth taken from sixty-four most disgusting places—we refrain from accompanying the Hindu author in his enumeration of the places in question—mingled with his enemy's hair and nail-clippings, small figures are made, upon whose bosom the name of the person upon whom it is desired to take revenge is inscribed. Magical words and mentrams are then pronounced over them, and they are consecrated by sacrifices. As soon as this is done, the grahas, or evil genii of the planets, take possession of the person who is the subject of animosity, and he is subjected to all sorts of evil treatment.

Sometimes these figures are transfixed with an awl, or are injured in various ways, with the object of really killing or disabling him who is the object of vengeance.

Sixty-four roots of various kinds of the most noxious plants are known to the magicians, which in their hands become the most powerful weapons for the secret infliction of the deadliest blows upon those at whom they are aimed.

Notwithstanding, the occupation of a magician is not without danger by any means. The gods and evil genii are very vindictive and never obey the injunctions of a miserable mortal very good-humoredly. It often happens that they punish him very severely for the brutal way in which he orders them about.

Woe to him if he makes the slightest mistake, if he is guilty of the most insignificant omission of the innumerable ceremonies which are obligatory upon him in the performance of an evocation. All the ills that were intended for others are incontinently showered down upon his own head.

He is constantly in fear, it seems, lest some other member of the same confraternity, of greater ability than himself, may succeed in making his own imprecations rebound upon himself or his patrons.

All these superstitious doctrines still exist in India, and most of the pagodas belonging to the vulgar cult possess, apart from the higher priests whom they are compelled to lodge and feed, a body of magicians whose services are let out to the lower castes, in precisely the same way as those of the Fakirs.

Now they undertake to rid a woman from the nocturnal embraces of an incubus: at another time they undertake to restore the virile power of a man where it has been lost in consequence of a spell cast by some opposing magician.

At other times, they are called upon to protect flocks, that have been decimated through the enchantments of others, against all noxious influences.

From time to time, in order to keep alive in the public

mind the belief in these sacred doctrines, these jugglers send out challenges to other pagodas, and publicly engage in contests, in the presence of witnesses and arbitrators, who are called in to decide which of the two champions is the more accomplished in his art.

The object of the contest is to obtain possession of an enchanted bit of straw, a small stick, or a piece of money.

The antagonists are both placed at the same distance from the object, whatever it may be, and they both make believe to approach it, but the mentrams they utter, the evocations they perform, the enchanted powders which they reciprocally throw at each other, possess a virtue which repels them: an invincible and overpowering force seems to stand in the way; they make fresh attempts to advance but they are forced back; they redouble their efforts; they fall into spasms and convulsions, they perspire profusely and spit blood. Ultimately one of them obtains possession of the enchanted object and is declared the victor.

It sometimes happens that one of the combatants is overthrown by the power of his adversary's mentrams. In that case he rolls on the ground as though he were possessed by a demon, and remains there motionless for some time, appearing to have lost his mind.

At last he recovers the use of his senses, arises in an apparent state of fatigue and exhaustion, and seems to retire covered with shame and confusion. He returns to the pagoda and does not make his appearance again for some time. A serious sickness is supposed to have ensued in consequence of the incredible, though ineffectual, efforts he has made.

There is no doubt that these pitiable farces, with which those who have been honestly initiated into the genuine worship of the Pitris are in no way connected whatever, are all concerted in advance, between the priests belonging to the vulgar cult of the rival pagodas and the charlatans by whom they are performed, and the victory is ascribed to each in turn. But the multitude who witness these spectacles, and who pay generously for them, are filled with fear and admiration of the sorcerers themselves, and are firmly persuaded that their contortions are due to supernatural causes.

There is one fact of which there can be no doubt, and that is, that these men perform their part with extraordinary truthfulness and expression, and that within the domain of pure magnetism they are really able to produce phenomena of which we have no idea in Europe. They are, however, inferior in ability to the Fakirs, belonging to the first class of initiates.

When, however, we come to consider the external manifestations by means of which the believers in the Pitris display their power, we shall look upon the performances of the magicians as trifling in comparison and unworthy of further consideration. They are obviously due to trickery and deception; we have already devoted quite enough space to them to give the reader an idea of what they can do.

There also exists in India another kind of enchantment, which is called *drichty-dotcha*, or a spell cast by the eyes. All animated beings, all plants, all fruits are subject to it. In order to remove it, it is customary to erect a pole in all gardens or cultivated fields, at the top of which is attached a large earthen vessel, the inside of which is whitened with whitewash: it is placed there, being a conspicuous and noticeable object, in order to attract the attention of any passing enemy, and thus prevent his looking at the crops, which would certainly be thereby injured.

We have rarely seen a rice-field in Ceylon or India that was not provided with one or more of these countercharms.

The Hindus are so credulous upon this point that they are continually fancying that they cannot perform a single act of their lives, or take a single step, however insignificant it may be, without danger of receiving from a neighbor, or a mere passer-by, or even a relative, the *drichty-dotcha.* There is nothing in the appearance of those who possess this fatal gift to indicate that they are so endowed. Those who have it are often unconscious of it themselves. For this reason every Hindu, several times a day, causes to be performed in the case of himself, his family, his fields, and his house, the ceremony of the *arratty*, the design of which is to counteract any harm that might otherwise befall him from spells cast by the eyes.

The *arratty* is one of their commonest practices, whether public or private. It may almost be elevated to the height of a national custom, so general is it in every province. It is always performed by women, and any woman is qualified to perform it except widows, who are never admitted to any domestic ceremony, their mere presence alone being unlucky.

The ceremony is performed as follows:

A lamp full of oil, perfumed with sandal-wood, is placed on a metal plate. It is then lighted, and one of the women of the household when her father, or husband, or any other member of the family, comes in from outdoors, takes the plate in her hand, and raises it as high as the head of the person upon whom the ceremony is to be performed, and describes therewith either three or seven circles according to his or her age or rank.

Instead of a lighted lamp, a vase is often used containing water perfumed with sandal-wood and saffron, reddened by vermilion, and consecrated by the immersion of a few stalks of the divine cousa grass.

The *arratty* is publicly performed several times a day upon persons of distinction, such as rajahs, provincial governors, army generals, or others of elevated rank. It is a ceremony to which courtiers are bidden, as formerly with us to the king's *levée.* One practice is quite as ridiculous to us as the other, and judging from what we have ourselves seen, in certain provinces in the Deccan, where the English have allowed a few phantoms of rajahs still to remain, the courtiers in this country are quite as degraded and servile a class as with us. They pay for the crumbs they receive and the favors they enjoy by the sacrifice of every feeling of conscience or dignity. It is the same everywhere. We must say, however, to the credit of the Hindu courtiers, that they never made their wives or daughters the mistresses of their rajahs.

As a general thing, a Hindu of any caste would blush to owe his own preferment to the dishonor of his wife.

Whenever persons belonging to a princely rank have been obliged to appear in public, or to speak to strangers, they never fail, upon returning to their palaces, to summon their wives or send for their devadassis from the neighboring temple to perform this ceremony upon them, and thus prevent the serious consequences that might otherwise result from any baleful glances to which they may have been exposed. They often have in their pay girls specially employed for that purpose.

Whenever you enter a Hindu house, if you are regarded as a person of distinction, the head of the family directs the young women to perform the ceremony of *arratty*. It is also performed for the statues of the gods.

When the dancing-girls at the temples have finished their other ceremonies, they never fail to perform the *arratty* two or three times over the gods to whose service they are attached.

This is also practised with still more solemnity when their statues are carried in procession through the streets. Its object is to avert any bad consequences resulting from glances which it is as difficult for the gods to avoid as simple mortals. Finally, the *arratty* is generally performed upon elephants, horses, domestic animals, and particularly upon the sacred bullocks, and even sometimes upon growing fields of rice.

Beside the more elevated doctrines taught by those who believe in the Pitris, vulgar magic in India takes its place as a degenerate descendant. It was the work of the lower priesthood and intended to keep the people in a constant state of apprehension. In all times, and in all places, by the side of the most elevated philosophical speculations, we always find the religion of the people.

We have dwelt at some length upon the practice of magic and sorcery in India, though they have nothing whatever to do with the higher worship which initiated Brahmins pay to the shades of their ancestors and the superior spirits, for the reason that nothing was better calculated to prove the Asiatic origin of most of the nations of Europe than a detailed description of these strange customs, which are identical with many that we meet with upon our own soil, and of which our historical traditions furnished us no explanation until we made the discovery that we were related to the Hindus by descent.

People in the middle ages believed implicitly in succubi and incubi, in the efficacy of magical formulas, in sorcery and the evil eye. Coming down to a period nearer our own times, we have not forgotten those fanatical *leaguers*, who carried their superstition to such a pitch that they used to make little images of wax representing Henry III. and the King of Navarre. They were accustomed to transfix these images in different places and keep them so for a period of forty days. On the fortieth day they stabbed them to the heart, fully persuaded that they would thus cause the death of the princes they were designed to represent. Practices of this kind were so common that, in 1571, a pretended sorcerer named Trois-Échelles, who was executed on the *Place de Grève*, declared in his examination that there were more than three thousand persons engaged in the same business, and that there was not a woman at court, or belonging to the middle or lower class, who did not patronize the magicians, particularly in love matters.

The execution of Gauffredy, the curé, and of Urbain Grandier, by Richelieu's orders, sufficiently demonstrate that the greatest minds of the time were not able to withstand the influence of these superstitions.

We read in Saint Augustine's Book, called "The City of God," that disbelief in the power of evil spirits was equivalent to a refusal to believe in the Holy Scriptures themselves.

The Bible, which is taken from the sacred books of antiquity, believed in sorcery, and the sorcerer must stand or fall with the authority of the Bible.

It is scarcely a century since persons convicted of magic were burnt at the stake, and we are struck with amazement by some of the sentences rendered by magistrates, still highly esteemed by their countrymen, according to which, upon the mere charge of sorcery, poor people suffered death by fire as charlatans, who, at the most, were only guilty of having cheated their neighbors out of a few sols by contrivances which were rather calculated to excite mirth than to do any serious injury.

It is difficult to understand these sentences, except by supposing that the magistrates themselves were in the occult power of the sorcerers.

In 1750, a Jesuit named Girard had a narrow escape from being burnt alive by a decree of the parliament of Provence, for having cast a spell upon the fair Cadière. He was saved by the disagreement of his judges, who were equally divided in opinion as to his guilt. He was given the benefit of the doubt.

A nun of the noble Chapter of Wurtzburg was burnt at the stake in the same year for being guilty of magical practices.

Since that time, fortunately, we have made some progress.

When we threw off the yoke of the Romish priest, from that day common sense, conscience, and reason resumed their sway, and while our Hindu ancestors, who are yet under the dominion of their Brahmins and Necromancers, still slumber on in the last stages of decrepitude and decay, we have made great strides in the path of scientific progress and intellectual liberty.

We always meet the priest and sorcerer upon the same plane of social charlatanism. They are both products of superstition and grow out of the same causes.

From an ethnographic point of view, it is interesting to observe that the Romans also inherited similar opinions from their Hindu ancestors.

We remember what Ovid said of Medea, the magician:

> Per tumulos erat passis discincta capillis,
> Certaque de tepidis colligit ossa rogis,
> Devovet absentes, simulacraque cerea fingit
> Et miserum tenues in jecur urget acus.

Horace also speaks of two magicians, named Canidia and Sagana, whose apparatus contained two figures, one of wool and the other of wax.

> . . . . Major
> Lanea, quæ pœnis compesceret inferiorem:
> Cerea suppliciter stabat: servilibus utque
> Jam peritura, modis.

We must confess, however, that the Lydian singer was not very much in earnest in speaking of them, when we consider the noise—*Proh pudor!*—by whose aid he caused them to be put to flight by the god of gardens, who was annoyed by their enchantments.

Horace would certainly not have sent his two witches to the stake.

The same ideas with regard to visual influences also existed among the Romans, as shown, among other things, by the following line from Virgil:

> Nescio quis teneros oculus mihi fascinat agnos.

They had their god Fascinus and their amulets of that name, which were designed to protect children from injury from that source. The statue of the same god, suspended from the triumphal car, was a protection to its occupants from any harm that might otherwise befall them from the *evil eye* of envy.

The object of the present work is not so much the study of magic in ancient times, as that of the more elevated religious beliefs, under whose guidance the vital atom successively progressed from one transformation to another, until it was absorbed in the Great All; which look upon the world of souls as being nothing but a succession of offspring and ancestors, who never forget each other: beliefs which indeed we may not entertain, but which are embalmed in a most mysterious and consolatory creed and are entitled to our respect.

The present chapter with regard to Hindu magic is merely an episode which we do not propose to extend further; otherwise we might show that the popular traditions with regard to sorcery in India found their way also into Greece, Rome, and ancient Chaldea.

One word hovever about this latter country, which, as claimed by Berosus, Æschylus, and Herodotus, was colonized by a multitude of unknown people and mixed tribes, speaking different languages.

India, with its hundred and twenty-five dialects and its various castes, so different from each other, was the only country, at that time, from which emigration was constantly going on, in order to avoid sacerdotal persecution, and from which, consequently, the countries bordering upon the Tigris and the Euphrates could possibly have been colonized.

To all the ethnographic facts, which go to show that the assertion here made is historically correct, may be further added the great similarity existing between the magical practices and beliefs of the Hindus and Chaldeans.

The following are some of the Assyrian inscriptions relating to magical enchantments, taken from a recent publication by Messrs. Rawlinson & Norris, which show how largely Chaldea was indebted to India.

"The form of the Chaldean conjurations against evil spirits," says the eminent Assyriologist, "is very monotonous. They are all cast in the same mould. They begin with a list of the demons to be overcome by the conjuration, together with a description of the character and effects of their power. This is followed by the expression of a desire to see them driven away, or of being protected from them, which is often presented in an affirmative form. The formula finally concludes with a mysterious invocation, from which it derives all its efficacy. 'Spirit of Heaven, remember; Spirit of Earth, remember.' That alone is necessary and never fails; but sometimes similar invocations to other divine spirits are also added.

"I will give as an example, one of these conjurations to be used against different bad demons, maladies, or acts, such as the *evil eye*.

—The pestilence, or fever, that lays waste the country. The plague that devastates the land, bad for the body, and injurious to the bowels.

—The bad demon, the bad Alal, the bad Gigim.

—The evil man, the evil eye, the evil mouth, the evil tongue, may they come out of the body, may they come out of the bowels of the man, son of his God.

—They shall never enter into possession of my body.

—They shall never do any harm before me. They shall never walk after me.

—They shall never enter into my house.

—They shall never cross my frame.

—They shall never enter the house of my habitation.

—Spirit of Heaven, remember! Spirit of Earth, remember!

—Spirit of Moul-ge, lord of countries, remember!
—Spirit of Nin-gelal, lady of countries, remember!
—Spirit of Nin-dar, powerful warrior of Moul-ge, remember!
—Spirit of Pa-kou, sublime intelligence of Moul-ge, remember!
—Spirit of En-zouna, eldest son of Moul-ge, remember!
—Spirit of Tiskou, lady of armies, remember!
—Spirit of Im, king whose impetuosity is beneficent, remember!
—Spirit of Oud, king of justice, remember!

"The following is another, where the final enumeration is not so long:

—The evening of evil omen, the region of heaven that produces misfortune,
—The fatal day, the region of the sky bad for observation,
—The fatal day, the bad region of the sky, that advances.
—Messengers of the plague,
—Ravagers of Nin-ki-gal,
—The thunder that rages throughout the country,
—The seven gods of the vast heavens,
—The seven gods of the vast earth,
—The seven gods of the fiery spheres,
—The seven malicious gods,
—The seven bad phantoms,
—The seven malicious phantoms of flames,
—The seven gods of heaven,
—The seven gods of the earth,
—The bad demon,
—The bad alal,
—The bad gigim,
—The bad tilol,

—The bad god, the bad maskim,
—Spirit of Heaven, remember!
—Spirit of Earth, remember!
—Sprit of Moul-ge, king of countries, remember!
—Spirit of Ningelal, lady of countries, remember?
—Spirit of Nin-dar, son of Zenith, remember!
—Spirit of Tishkou, lady of countries, who shines in the night, remember!

"More commonly, however, there are no such mythological enumerations at the end. As an example of the more simple kind of formulas, I may mention a conjuration against the seven subterranean demons, called maskim, who were reckoned among the most formidable of any.

—The seven! the seven!
—At the lowest bottom of the abyss, the seven!
—Abomination of heaven! the seven!
—Hiding themselves in the lowest depths of heaven and earth,
—Neither male nor female,
—Water, stretched out captives,
—Having no wives and producing no children,
—Knowing neither order nor good,
—Hearing no prayer,
—Vermin, that hidest in the mountain,
—Enemies of the god Ea,
—Ravagers of the gods,
—Abettors of trouble,
—All-powerful by violence,
—Agents of enmity,
—Spirit of Heaven, remember!
—Spirit of Earth, remember!"

We shall dwell no further upon this point, however. The above inscriptions are superabundant proof that the practice of magic, as handed down to the ancient Chaldeans from their ancestors, the Hindu emigrants of the lower castes or mixed classes, as Berosus calls them, was the utmost limit of their attainments in that direction.

The pure doctrines, which formed the subject of initiation, the worship of the Pitris and the superior spirits, awoke no echo upon the banks of the Euphrates. The nomads and brick moulders of the Sennar country lived in constant apprehension of the sorcerers and magicians, with no idea even of the existence of the sublime conceptions of Brahminism.

Inscriptions recorded upon granite, marble, stone, or baked earth, invariably contain everything that is most elevated in the popular belief. We do not select the superstitious ideas of the multitude to bequeath to future ages, and, as it were, to immortalize them.

I am all and in all!

says the Trinitarian inscription at Elephanta, in India.

I have begotten the world!

says the record upon the statue of Isis, which was the emblem of mother Nature in Egypt.

Know thyself!

such was the inscription that appeared in front of the temple at Delphi.

And the column erected in the Agora at Athens was inscribed:

To the unknown God!

Mingling in their inscriptions their gods and evil spirits, such as the gigim, the maskim, and other demons, trembling with constant fear in the presence of sexless, wifeless, and childless monsters, before these telals, these ravagers of heaven, these enemies of Ea, the King of the Gods, who also seemed to tremble in their presence, the Chaldeans engraved upon their burnt bricks nothing but expressions of the grossest superstition, for the simple reason that they had nothing else to put there. If there is any one thing at which we have a right to express our surprise, it is that some Assyriologists have taken these ridiculous conceptions as a text from which to prove that the ancient Hindus got their first ideas from the primitive Chaldeans.

The Agrouchada-Parikchai, in a fourth book, which we have already alluded to, in which it gives an account of the magic practices, whereby bad spirits are set in motion, but which is entirely ineffectual as far as the Pitris, or the superior spirits, or Swayambhouva, the Supreme Being, are concerned, and which fourth book is entirely disconnected from the other three, which are wholly devoted to the pure doctrine of the Pitris, makes no secret of the fact that magic and sorcery were the only things that had any influence upon the impure Soudras, or the common people and Tchandalas, or mixed classes.

Before passing on to the subject of the phenomena and external manifestations produced by those who had gone through the various degrees of initiation in India, it may not be amiss to compare the doctrine of the Pitris, as we have set it forth, with the beliefs of the Jewish cabalists and of several other philosophers of ancient times, who seem to us to have drank from the same fountain.

PART THIRD.

THE DOCTRINE OF THE PITRIS AS COMPARED WITH THAT OF THE JEWISH CABALA, OF PLATO, OF THE ALEXANDRIAN SCHOOL, OF PHILO, OF THE PERSIANS, AND OF CHRISTIANITY.

It is not lawful to explain the history of creation to two persons, or the history of the Mercaba even to one. If, however, he is naturally a wise and intelligent man, he may be intrusted with the heads of the chapters. (Extract from the Mischna, a Jewish cabalistic work, portions of which were translated by A. Franck of the Institute.)

* * *

As for the ten Sephiroth, there is no end, either in the future, or in the past, nor in good or evil, nor in depth or height, nor in the east, west, north, or south. The ten Sephiroth are like the fingers of the hands to the number of ten, five on either side, but at the middle lays the point of unity.

Keep your mouth closed that you may not speak of it, and your heart that you may not think of it; and if your heart forgets itself, bring it back again to its place, for that is the reason why the union was formed. (Sephir Jéoziroh, a cabalistic work, translated by A. Franck, of the Institute.)

THE DOCTRINE OF THE PITRIS

AND

THE JEWISH CABALA.

CHAPTER I.

ORIGIN OF THE CABALA.

In opposition to the outward observances with which the prescriptions of the Bible are encumbered under the Jewish law, by which all intelligent action, all freedom of the will are crushed out, there arose gradually by its side, in response to a demand for a greater independence of thought, and a wider philosophy, a mysterious doctrine which was known by the name of the Jewish Cabala.

Those who believed in this doctrine, the object of which was to unfold the secrets of the divine nature, as well as of the creation, wrapped themselves up in silence and mystery like initiates in the Indian temples. At distant intervals, says the illustrious Franck, in his admirable book upon this mystic philosophy,[1] with innumerable precautions they partly opened the doors of the sanctuary to some new adept, who was always chosen among those particularly eminent for their intellectual ability, and whose advanced age offered an additional proof of their wisdom and discretion.

[1] The Cabala, or Religious Philosophy of the Jews.

When a new candidate was initiated into the mysteries of the Cabala, one of the elders murmured in his ears the following words:

"O thou who hast now gone to the fountain-head of all the graces, be careful, whenever tempted to do so, not to reveal the tenet of emanation, which is a great mystery in the judgment of all Cabalists. Another mystery is contained in the following words: 'Thou shalt not tempt the Lord.'"

The necessity of a special initiation, an essential prerequisite of which was that the candidate should be far advanced toward the close of life, and the absolute secrecy which the person initiated was expected to preserve with regard to whatever was revealed to him, were two points of external discipline, in respect to which those who held to the doctrine of the Pitris in India, and the believers in the Jewish Cabala were very nearly agreed, though, in matters of belief, we shall soon see they were united by ties that bound them still closer to each other. In all times science has anxiously sought to discover the origin of the philosophical system of the Hebrews, which presents many points of resemblance with some of the Greek systems of Alexandria and with the mystical beliefs of Arabia.

As the Cabala is manifestly older than the Alexandrian school, it cannot be successfully held to have sprung from the latter, though it may have been influenced by it to some extent. The most that can be claimed is that both systems have drunk from the same source. As for the close connection that seems to exist between it and the mystical philosophy of the Arabs, we may well ask, with Messrs. Franck and Tholuck, who have investigated the subject in all its bearings, "What conclusion are we to draw from these many points of resemblance?"

"They are not of much importance, it is true, for what is similar in both systems is to be found elsewhere in more ancient systems. In the books of the Sabeans and Persians, for instance, and also among the Neo-Platonists. On the other hand, the extraordinary form under which these ideas are presented to us in the Cabala is unlike that of the Arab mystics. In order to satisfy ourselves that the Cabala really sprang from intercourse with the latter, we should find among them some traces of the doctrine of the Zephiroth. But not a vestige of it is to be met with. They knew of but one form under which God reveals himself to himself. In this respect the Cabala is much more like the doctrine of the Sabeans and Gnostics.

"No trace, either, is to be found among the Arabs of the doctrine of metempsychosis, which occupies such a prominent position in the Hebrew system. We also search their books in vain for the allegories we are constantly meeting with in the Zohar, for those continual appeals to tradition, for those daring and multitudinous personifications with their endless genealogies, and for those astonishing and extraordinary metaphors which harmonize so well with the spirit of the East."

These multitudinous incarnations and interminable genealogies, or, in other words, these men elevating themselves to the infinite by the improvement of their spiritual nature; this belief in the doctrine of metempsychosis, and the tenet relating to the ten Zephiroth, or the creative faculty of the divinity; such are the recognized bases of the Cabalistic philosophy.

We have seen that the belief in the doctrine of the Pitris is based on similar principles. The ten Zephiroth of the Hebrews are substantially the same as the ten Pradjapatis of India, to whom all creatures are indebted for their existence.

The Zohar, which is the principal work of the Cabala, speaking of the philosophical system therein taught, says that it is precisely the same as the wisdom which the children of the East have known from the earliest times.

"Evidently," says Franck, "this cannot refer to the Arabs, whom the Hebrew writers invariably call *the children of Israel, or the children of Arabia:* they would not speak of a foreign and contemporaneous philosophy in such terms—the Zohar would not date it back from the earliest ages of the world."

While the origin of the Cabala cannot be successfully sought for either in the different systems of Greece or in the doctrines of the Alexandrian school, notwithstanding they have many points in common, or in the mystical philosophy of the Arabs; while, on the other hand, the Zohar, tracing it back to the earliest ages, speaks of it as having the East for its cradle; have we not good reason, therefore, in view of the antiquity of India and the similarity in principle of both systems, to say that the doctrine of the Cabala sprang from the doctrine of the Pitris?

We should not forget that India, that immense and luminous centre in olden times, besides spreading its ideas throughout the East, by means of emigration, from the earliest times, was in constant communication with all the people of Asia, and that all the philosophers and sages of antiquity went there to study the science of life. It is not, therefore, surprising that in periods of their captivity the elders of the Hebrews should have been initiated by the Persian Magi into the old conceptions of the Brahmins.

A few extracts from the Sepher Jeszireh and the Zohar, the two highest prized works of the Cabala, as to the nature of God, the creation, and the human soul, will show conclusively that this opinion is historically correct.

We shall be brief, for while we cannot resist the temptation to devote a few pages to the subject of these comparisons, we shall bear in mind that we cannot dwell upon it at any great length, except at the expense of our main subject.

CHAPTER II.

HOW THE SACRED BOOKS ARE TO BE INTERPRETED ACCORDING TO THE JEWISH CABALISTS.

In order to show that these things are not to be taken in their literal signification, and that they have a hidden meaning which is contained therein, as in a seed, and has to be extracted from them, the Zohar repeats the following allegory:

Picture to yourself a man living alone in the mountain and unacquainted with the usages of the city. He produced and lived upon wheat, which he ate in its natural state.

One day he went to the city, where he was given some bread of good quality. He asked:

What is this good for?

He was answered,

It is bread to eat.

He took it and liked it, after which he asked again,

What is it made of?

The answer was,

It is made of wheat.

Some time afterward he was given some cakes mixed with oil. He tasted them and asked:

And what is this made of, pray?

He was answered

It is made of wheat.

By-and-by some royal pastry mixed with oil and honey was set before him.

He asked the same question as before.

What is this?

He was answered, they are cakes made of wheat.

He exclaimed,

All these things are at my command. I use them already in their crude state; I use the wheat of which they are made.

So thinking, he was a total stranger to the pleasures they give, which were all lost to him. So it is with those who give their whole attention to the general principles of science, and are ignorant of the pleasures therefrom resulting.

The Zohar concludes as follows: "It is necessary to extract from the letter of the law, the charms of wisdom that are therein hidden."

We find also the following aphorisms in the same book.

* * *

Wo to the man who does not look beyond the letter of the law, but regards it as simply a record of events in ordinary language.

* * *

The words of the law are the garments, in which it is clothed. Wo to him who takes the garment of the law for the law itself.

* * *

There are some foolish people who, seeing a man covered with a handsome garment, never look any further, but take this garment for the body, while there is something which is more precious, and that is the soul.

* * *

The law also has its body. There are commandments which may be called the body of the law; the texts that are mingled with them are merely the garments by which they are covered.

Ordinary people pay heed to nothing but the garments, or to the texts of the law. That is all they know. They see nothing that is hidden beneath this garment. Those who are wiser pay no heed to the garment, but to the body by which it is enveloped.

* * *

The servants of the Supreme King, those who live upon the heights of Sinai, heed nothing but the soul, which is the basis of everything else, which is the law itself, and, in future times, they will be prepared to contemplate the soul of that soul which is manifested through the law.

By treating the sacred books in this allegorical way, the Cabalists, without doing violence to the Bible or tradition, made the conceptions which were the subject of initiation in ancient times in the East, a part of their religious law.

These last verses seem like a commentary upon the same subject as that which we have been considering, taken from the Book of the Pitris.

We merely call attention to the similarity between the two methods of interpretation, adopted by the adherents of either doctrine, without dwelling upon it any further.

We are reminded of what was said in the Agrouchada-Parikchai:

" As the soul is contained in the body;

" As the almond is concealed by its envelope;

" As the sun is veiled by the clouds;

" As the garments hide the body from sight;

" As the egg is included in its shell;

" And as the germ rests inside of the seed;

" So the sacred law has its body, its envelope, its clouds, its garments, its shell, which hide it from the knowledge of the multitude."

This opinion, that the words of the law were nothing but garments intended to conceal from the common people ths truths therein contained, led the Cabalists to construct what they called a Cabalistic alphabet, by whose aid they even prevented the material act of reading their mysteries.

According to Reuchlin, "De Arte Cabalistic.," and Wolf, "Bibligr. Hebr.," the method employed in that occult alphabet in order to make it necessary that the mere act of reading should be the subject of a special initiation, was tri-fold.

The first consisted of the substitution of one word for another, to which it was equivalent.

According to the second, the final letter of each word became the initial of another word.

The third changed the value of the letters by putting, for instance, the first in place of the last, and *vice-versa*.

We have seen that those who believed in the Indian doctrine of the Pitris also indulged in these puerile practices.

CHAPTER III.

INITIATION AMONG THE CABALISTS.

We have seen that the mysteries taught in the Indian pagoda comprised three degrees of initiation, in each of which a probation of twenty years was required before being promoted to a higher grade.

The writers on the Cabala have not given us all the secrets of their interior discipline, but there is no doubt that the Hebraic initiation also included several categories.

It is well known, according to the Talmud, that the ancient Hebrews had three names to express the idea of God.

The first, which was composed of four letters, was taught to all who came for instruction to the temple.

With regard to the second and third, which consisted of twelve and forty-two letters respectively, the following are the words of Maimonides:

"Sages taught the name of twelve letters to their sons and disciples; but when the number of the ungodly had increased, it was intrusted only to the most discreet among the priests, and they repeated it in a low tone to their brethren, while the people were receiving the benediction."

The name of forty-two letters was the most sacred of all mysteries. It contained the great secret of the universal soul, and stood for, if we may so express it, the highest degree of initiation.

"It was only taught," says the author whom we have just quoted, "to a man of recognized discretion, of mature age, not addicted to anger or intemperance, a stranger to vanity, and gentle and pleasant with all with whom he was brought into contact."

"Whoever," says the Talmud, "has been made acquainted with this secret and vigilantly keeps it in a pure heart, may reckon upon the love of God and the favor of men; his name inspires respect; his knowledge is in no danger of being forgotten, and he is the heir of two worlds, that in which we live, and the world to come."

These three classes of persons, viz.:

First, the disciples, who were taught the name consisting of four letters:

Second, the priests, who studied that of twelve letters; and

Third, the elders, to whom alone the secret of the forty-two letters was revealed,

—seem to us to correspond very closely to the three grades of initiation in India.

It is worthy of remark, according to the last quotation from the Talmud, that the elders who are in possession of this most sacred mystery, are invested with supreme power, not only in the present world but in the world of invisible spirits.

In the Zohar, in the Sepher Jeszirah, in the Guemara, and in the Mischna we are constantly meeting with the prohibition to divulge the secrets of the Mercaba, or creation, to anybody except,

"Men who are invested with the highest dignity and who are known for their extreme prudence."

"Whose heart," according to the original expression, "is filled with anxiety and alarm."

From a text which we quoted in the first chapter of the first part of this work, it appears that a distinguished position, with respect to intellect and accomplishments, was not all that was required from him who aspired to a knowledge of these mysteries, but that he must also have arrived at a certain age.

The Rabbi Jochanan one day said to the Rabbi Eleazar: "Let me teach you the history of the Mercaba." The latter answered, "I am not old enough for that." When he had grown old enough, the Rabbi Jochanan was dead. Some time afterward, the Rabbi Assi said to him in his turn, "Let me teach you the history of the Mercaba." He replied: "If I had deemed myself worthy, I should have learnt it before, from the Rabbi Jochanan, your master."

Though we may not be able to point out the special practices observed by those who had been initiated into the mysteries of the Jewish Cabala, as they were promoted from one degree to a higher, owing to the silence of their traditions and written works upon that subject, still, we have reason to think, at any rate, that as in India there were three degrees of initiation.

CHAPTER IV.

THE DIVINE ESSENCE, ACCORDING TO THE CABALISTS.

Rabbi Simon, having assembled his disciples, seated himself beneath the shade of a sacred forest, and informed them that, before dying, he would reveal to them the great secret of the principle of principles.

"A voice was then heard and their knees shook together for fright. What was that voice? It was the voice of the celestial assembly (including all the superior spirits) which had assembled to listen. Rabbi Simon joyfully spoke as follows: O Lord! I will not say, like one of thy prophets, that upon hearing thy voice I was afraid, for this is not the time to be afraid, but it is the time for love, as it is written: Thou shalt love the eternal, thy God."

The Zohar then puts into his mouth the following description of the Supreme Being:

"He is the Ancient of ancients, the mystery of mysteries, the unknown of those who are unknown. He has a form that appertains to him, inasmuch as he appears to us as a man far advanced in life, as the Ancient of ancients, as whatever is most unknown among those who are unknown, but under this form beneath which he manifests himself to us, he still remains unknown, his garment seems white, and his aspect is that of one whose face is exposed; he is seated upon a throne of thunderbolts, which he uses at pleasure. The white light of his head lights up four hundred thousand worlds. Four hundred thousand worlds, springing from this white light, are the inheritance of the just in the world to come. Every day witnesses the birth of thirteen thousand myriads of worlds which receive their subsistence from him, and the burthen of which is entirely supported by him. A refreshing dew drops from his head, which awakes the dead and infuses into them a new life, wherefore it is written; Thy dew is a dew of light; it is the food of the highest order of spirits; it is the manna which is prepared for the just in the life to come. It drops upon the field of sacred fruit. In appearance this dew seems white like diamonds, whose color contains all colors. The length of his face, from the summit of his head is three hundred and seventy times ten thousand worlds. He is called the long-face, for such is the name of the Ancient of ancients."

"Before he created any form in this world, before he produced any image, he was alone, without form, resembling nothing. Who can conceive of him as he was then, previous to creation, inasmuch as he had no form? Therefore it is not lawful to represent him by means of any image or under any form whatever, even by his holy name, even by a letter or a point. Such is the meaning of the words. You saw no figure on the day when the Eternal spoke to us."

"Woe to him who ventures to compare him even to one of his own attributes; much less still should he be compared to man who springs from the earth, and whose destiny is death. He should be conceived of as above all creatures and all attributes."

"Learn, however, that no one is intelligent or wise, except of his own substance, for wisdom does not deserve the name by itself, but on account of him who is wise, and who produces it from the light emanating from himself. Moreover, no one can conceive of intelligence as existing by itself alone, but through him who is an intelligent being and who fills it with his own substance." (Extract from the Zohar, a Cabalistic work.)

"The Ancient of ancients is, at the same time, the most unknown of unknown beings. He is distinct from everything, and yet he is not separated from anything; for everything is united to him as he is united to everything; there is nothing that is not in him. He has a form and we may say that he has none. Upon assuming a form he gave existence to everything that is. In the first place, he projected from his own bosom ten luminaries—or the ten Zephiroth—which shine by the form they borrowed from him, and diffuse on all sides a most brilliant light. In the same manner as a beacon spreads rays of lights everywhere around it, the Ancient of ancients, the unknown of all unknown beings, is an elevated beacon, which we know merely by the light, which shines in our eyes with such brilliancy and fulness. What we call his holy name is only this light." (Extract from the Idra-Souata, a Cabalistic work.)

"The Ancient of ancients, whose name be sanctified, is the only form that embraces all other forms. It is supreme and mysterious wisdom, that includes everything." (Extract from the Zohar.)

These extracts contain almost everything that has been written by the Cabalists with regard to the divine nature, and we may say, indeed, that their whole system of philosophical belief is contained in its turn, in the following sayings, taken from the Book of the Pitris:

He is *all* and *in all*
And everything is in him!
He is the cause of everything and every effect is in him.

The same pantheism, in an infinite unity, was taught in the works of the Cabala as by those who had been initiated in the Indian temples. The Ancient of Ancients in the Zohar is precisely the same as the Ancient of Days in Manu, the Vedas, and the Agrouchada-Parikchai. We find the same fundamental ideas at the basis of both philosophies, expressed in almost identical terms.

We shall now show how this most unknown of unknown beings revealed himself in creation.

CHAPTER V.

THE TEN ZEPHIROTH.

The ten Zephiroth represent the ten essential qualities, by means whereof the deity is manifested in creation.

These ten attributes, representing goodness, glory, wisdom, power, grace, justice, intelligence, sovereignty, etc., are completely identified with the divine substance, but as God is immutable and is not susceptible of change, the Cabalists always regard him as in action, and the ten Zephiroth as instruments of the Supreme Power, as creatures of a superior nature, as types of all beings.

This is the way in which God reveals himself, and passes from evocation into action.

We will now yield the floor to the illustrious Hebraist whom we have adopted as our guide, and who can furnish a more correct description of this conception than we are able to give ourselves.

"God," says Franck, is "present in the Ten Zephiroth; otherwise he could not reveal himself through them; but he does not abide wholly in them; he is not solely what we are able to find out about him, through these sublime forms of thought and life. In point of fact, the Zephiroth can never comprehend the infinite. The En-Soph, which is the very source of all these forms, and which, in that capacity, has no form, or rather, to speak more correctly, while each Zephiroth has a well-known name, he alone has none and can have none."

God then remains the ever ineffable, incomprehensible, and infinite being, whose place is above that of all the worlds which reveal his presence to us, even the world of emanation.

Such is, likewise, the particular nature of each of the ten Pradjapatis of India, and the character of their relations toward Swayambhouva, the unrevealed being.

The analogy between them is so close and striking that any comments we might make would only weaken the force of their resemblance.

According both to the Cabalists and the believers in the Pitris, the Zephiroth and the ten Pradjapatis, who are the lords of creatures, are the attributes of divinity, as embodied in the Ten Superior Spirits, who manifest themselves in creation, and in this manner, the doctrine of the immutability of the Deity, who was only able to reveal himself in action, was not infringed upon in the slightest degree.

The close similarity between these beliefs, in India and Judea, is the more worthy of remark, inasmuch as we meet them in no other philosophical system at that period, and it incontestably indicates how closely the Hindu and Jewish systems are related to each other. This system was not fully set forth in the Cabala much more than a century previous to our era, while Manu, the Vedas, and the Agrouchada-Parikchai had already been in existence for several thousand years.

It may not be amiss to remark also that these Ten Superior Spirits, like the Indian Pradjapatis, are at the head of the immense hierarchy of spirits, both inspiring as well as mediating, who preside over the continual transformations of the vital molecule, and under whose guidance the human soul advances from one degree of perfection to another until it reaches the universal soul.

The Sepher Jeszirah speaks in the following enigmatical manner of these superior manifestations.

"There are ten Zephiroth, ten and not nine, ten and not eleven. Act so that you may intelligently understand them in your wisdom, so that your mind, your speculations, your knowledge, and your thoughts may be constantly engaged in their investigation. Let every thing rest upon its foundation and reinstate the Creator upon his basis.

"As for the Ten Zephiroth, there is no end, neither in the future nor in the past, nor in good nor evil, nor in height nor depth, nor in the east nor the west, nor in the south, nor in the north.

"The Ten Zephiroth are like the five fingers of each hand to the number of ten, five on either hand, but between them is the tie of unity.

"The end of the Zephiroth is united to the beginning, as the flame is united to the firebrand, for the Lord is one, and there is not a second.

"Close your mouth that you may not speak of it, and your heart that you may not think of it, and if your heart forgets itself, bring it to its place again, for it is for this reason that they have been united together." (Extract from the Sepher Jeszireh.)

Was not the meaning of the Agrouchada-Parikchai precisely identical, when it said, centuries before the Cabala was in existence:

"As for the Ten Pradjapatis, who are the lords of all created beings, and who are Maritchi, Atri, Angiras, Poulastya, Poulaha, Cratou, Pratchetas, Vasichta, Brighou, Narada, there is no commencement or end, neither in time nor space, for they are the product of the only essence of one spirit at a single breath.

"This is a fatal secret; close thy mouth that no part of it may be revealed to the vulgar herd; compress thy brain in order that no part of it may be spread abroad."

We will say in conclusion that the whole doctrine of the Pitris consists in a knowledge of that vast spiritual hierarchy at the head of which stand the Pradjapatis.

In like manner, the whole of the Jewish Cabala may be summed up as consisting in the mystic knowledge of the Zephiroth.

CHAPTER VI.

THE CABALISTIC TRINITY.

"Having divided his body into two parts, the sovereign ruler became half male and half female, and uniting with the female portion, begot Viradj the son." (Manu, sloca 34, book i.)

"I, Viradj, desiring to give birth to the human race, first produced the Ten Pradjapatis, who are the Lords of all created beings, after having practised the greatest austerities." (Manu, sloca 34, book i.)

In such terms as these, the venerable legislator of the Hindus first spake of the primitive triad, from which sprang the ten superior spirits, who first manifested themselves in creation.

We have already seen in what affecting language the Book of the Pitris speaks of the love of the husband for his spouse, and how the universe sprang from that celestial union. In all the pagodas of India, that symbolical trinity is represented by three heads, carved from a single block of granite or marble, in the form of a single head.

It is extraordinary to see how closely this idea, which sprang up on the banks of the Ganges, was copied in the teachings of the Jewish Cabalists.

We are free to confess that what we have said about the Cabala is not derived from our own knowledge upon that subject. All our information about the Hebrews is taken from Mr. Franck of the Institute, and the reader will understand that thereon rests the whole weight of our argument.

After this digression, we will now go on with our proofs. They seem like demonstrations in mathematics. We proposed to show that the Hebraic Cabala sprang originally from the Hindu temples. The best means at our command, in order to elucidate this problem, which is also interesting from an ethnographic point of view, is simply to confront the doctrine of the Pitris, as we have unfolded it, and the Hindu text, as we have given it, with the Hebraic texts themselves. We have also given the views of an eminent author, who certainly was not thinking of India when he was explaining the mysteries of the Zohar and the Sepher Jeszireh, and who too was wondering what could have been the birthplace of these extraordinary doctrines, which, in spite of certain points of similarity, never grew out of the Grecian or Arabic philosophies.

The following are the exact words of the Zohar, as given by the author in question, accompanied by his comments thereon. They lead from unity to the dyad, and from the dyad to the triad, by the same path which the thinkers in the Hindu pagodas had previously explored:

"In the beginning, was the Ancient. Seen face to face, he is the supreme head, the source of all light, the principle of all wisdom. The only definition that can be applied to him is, unity."

From the bosom of this absolute unity, of which, however, variety is a distinguishing feature, and from all relative unity, issue two principles in parallel lines, which are apparently opposed to each other, but in reality are not incompatible. The male, or active principle is called wisdom; the female, or passive principle is designated by a word that is commonly translated as intelligence.

"Everything that exists," says the Zohar, "everything that has been formed by the *Ancient*, whose name be sanctified, can only subsist through a *male* and a *female*."

From their eternal and mysterious union springs a *son*,

who, according to the original expression, takes after his *father* and *mother* together, and bears witness to both of them.

This son of wisdom and intelligence, called, on account of his double inheritance, the elder son of God, is knowledge, or science. *These three persons* contain and include everything that is, but they are united, in their turn, in the White Head, in the Ancient of ancients, for *all is he* and *he is all.*

Sometimes he is represented with three heads forming a single one. Sometimes he is compared to the brain, which, without losing its unity, is divided into three parts, and by means of thirty-two pairs of nerves is in communication with every part of the body, as, by the aid of the thirty-two methods of wisdom, the divinity is diffused throughout the universe.

"The Ancient," says the Zohar, "whose name be sanctified, exists with three heads forming a single one, and this head is the most elevated of all elevated things, and because the Ancient is represented by the number three, all the other lights, or, in other words, the ten Zephiroth, are also comprised within the number three."

In another part of the same work we read:

"There are three heads carved one within the other, and one above the other. In this number we reckon first hidden wisdom, which is never without a veil. This mysterious wisdom is the supreme principle of all other wisdom. Above this first head is the Ancient; whatever is most mysterious among mysteries. Finally comes the head which towers above all others, and which is no head. What it contains no one knows, or can know, for it equally escapes our knowledge and our ignorance. That is the reason why the Ancient is called the non-being."

Sometimes the terms or, if it is preferred, the persons of this trinity are represented as three successive and absolutely necessary phases of existence, as well as of thought, as a deduction or evolution which, at the same time, constitutes the generation of the world. However surprising it may seem, there can be no doubt about it, when we read the following lines taken from the Zohar:

"Come and see; thought is the principle of everything; but it is at first ignorant and self-contained. When thought succeeds in diffusing itself abroad it has reached that stage when it becomes spirit. When it has arrived at that point it is called intelligence, and is no longer contained within itself as before. The spirit develops itself, in its turn, among the mysteries by which it is surrounded, and a voice comes from it, which is like a reunion of the celestial choirs, a voice which is distinctly heard in articulate words, for it comes from the spirit, but when we think of all these degrees, we see that thought and intelligence, this voice and this language, are one and the same thing; that thought is the principle of everything that is, and that no interruption can exist therein. Thought itself is united to the non-being, and is never separated from it. Such is the meaning of the words; Jehovah is one and his name is one.

"The name, which signifies I am, indicates to us the union of everything that is, the degree where all the methods of wisdom are still hidden, and placed together, without our being able to distinguish one from the other, but when a line of demarkation is once established, when it is desired to distinguish the mother, *carrying all things in her womb, and upon the point* of giving birth to them, in order to reveal the supreme name; then God says, speaking of himself: *I who am.* Finally, *when all is carefully formed and has issued from the maternal womb*, when everything is in its place, and it is proposed both to designate the individual and existence, God calls himself Jehovah, or I am that which is."

We will conclude the present sketch by presenting a most extraordinary resemblance between the doctrine of the Pitris and that of the Jewish Cabalists.

In the Hindu system, as we have seen, there were three trinities which proceeded successively from Swayambhouva, *the self-existent being*, and were mingled in him *in a supreme union.* They are:

First, the initial trinity, which gave birth to the divine thought:

Nara, the producer,
Nari, the mother,
Viradj, the son.

Second, the trinity, as manifested, from which spring the primitive elements, which aid in the formation of the universe.

Agni,
Aya,
Sourya.

Third, the creating trinity:

Brahma,
Vishnou,
Siva.

Franck informs us, upon the authority of the Zohar, that a precisely similar doctrine was held by the Cabalists. He says:

"The ten Zephiroth were divided into *three classes.* Each presents the *divinity to us under a different aspect,* but always under the aspect of an *invisible trinity.*

"The first three Zephiroth are purely intellectual. As a matter of metaphysics, they express the absolute identity of thought and existence, and form what modern Cabalists call the intelligible world. It is the first manifestation of the Deity.

"*The three* that succeed them have a moral character: on the one hand, they make us conceive of God as identical with goodness and wisdom; on the other hand, they exhibit the Supreme Being as the origin of beauty and magnificence *in creation.* For this reason, they have been called the *virtues*, or the *sensible world.*

"Finally, we learn *by the last three Zephiroth* that the universal providence, or the Supreme Artist, is also *absolute force* or all-powerful cause, and that this cause is, at the same time, the *generating element of everything that is.* It is the last Zephiroth that constitutes the *natural world* or *nature*, in its *essence* and *active principle, natura naturans.*"

Upon prosecuting our inquiries as to the original source of the philosophical ideas of mankind, it is highly suggestive, to say the least of it, that the Brahminical and Cabalistic notion of the three trinities was almost identically the same.

First, there was an unrevealed God, the primordial and universal germ, the Ancient of Days, as he was called by the Hindus, the Ancient of Ancients, according to the Cabalistic philosophy.

Second, there was then a first trinity, begotten of thought and will.

Third, there was in either case a second trinity, which was the origin of the elements, of the virtues, and of the forces of the sensible world.

Fourth, according to the Hindus, a third trinity had charge of the work of creation; according to the Cabalists, it *represents the generative element of everything that is.*

Finally, in both doctrines, the active generative element, by perpetual union with the passive or mother element, was continually shooting into space the rays of life, from which souls escape and accomplish their progressive destinies in the universe, and gradually ascend and are absorbed in the immortal source from which they originally spring, or, in other words, in unity.

In order to give a clearer idea of this notion of the Great All, with its two-fold nature, continually begetting everything that exists, and of the universe which is the product, or offspring, perpetually ascending to unity, like the links of an endless chain, or a self-feeding flame, the Zohar makes use of the following comparison:

"In order to master the science of the sacred unity, look at the flame which rises from a brightly burning fire, or from a lighted lamp; first we see two lights, the one brilliantly white, the other black or blue. The white light is above the other, and rises in a straight line. The black light is underneath and seems to be the source of the former. They are, however, so closely united to each other that they form but one flame, but the foundation, formed by the blue or black light, in its turn, is connected with the burning matter which is still farther beneath. It should be known that the white light never changes; it always preserves its peculiar color, but several shades are distinguished in that which is beneath. The latter besides tends in two opposite directions. On top it is connected with the white light and below with the burning flame, but this matter is being continually absorbed in its bosom, and is continually ascending toward the superior light. In this manner everything returns to unity."

In view of the extraordinary similarity which we have shown to exist between the doctrines held by the Hindus and those of the Jewish Cabalists, what becomes of the claims of those Semitists who, in imitation of Renan, adopt every method to disseminate their peculiar views, independently of the fact that identically the same opinions were held by other people in Asia and the East.

CHAPTER VII.

THE BELIEF IN MEDIATING AND INSPIRING SPIRITS ACCORDING TO THE JEWISH CABALISTS.

"The inferior world has been created in the similitude of the superior. Everything that exists in the superior world appears here below like the reflection of an image, and yet it is all only one thing." (The Zohar.)

"It is needful for you to know that there is the same relation between the shadow and the body, as between the corporeal and spiritual worlds." (Al Gazali, a Cabalistic writer.)

The extraordinary similarity existing between the doctrines taught in the Indian pagodas and those of the Jewish Cabalists, was not, however, confined to their metaphysical conceptions. The Cabalists, as we shall show, also believed in mediating and inspiring spirits, and their belief was nothing but the logical consequence of the principles they held. The whole of creation, the entire universe, being merely a radiation from the divine nature, infinite space is peopled with spirits which have dropped, on the one hand, from the great all in the condition of sparks, or atoms, endowed with life, and who, on the other hand, are returning to it through a constant series of progressive transformations.

This condition of affairs is clearly unfolded in the Zohar, in the form of the following allegory:

"Spirits or the souls of the just," says that celebrated work, "are above all powers. If you ask why from a place so exalted they descend to the earth, so far away from their source, this is my answer: Their case is like that of a king, to whom a son was born, and who took him into the country, to be there reared and educated until he had grown older, and had been instructed in the customs of his father's palace. When the king was informed that his son's education was finished, what does his love for him prompt him to do? He sends for the queen, his mother, to celebrate his return. He brings him back to the palace, where the whole day is spent in rejoicing. The saint also had a son by the queen, blessed be his name. This son is the superior and sacred soul. He sends him to the country, or, in other words, into the world, to grow up and become acquainted with the usages of his father's palace. When it comes to the knowledge of the Ancient of Ancients that his son is grown, and that the time has come to introduce him into his presence, what does his love then prompt him to do? As a mark of honor, he sends for the queen, and brings her son home to his palace. Indeed, the soul has no sooner left the earth than the queen joins him, to show him the way to the king's palace, where she dwells forever and ever. And yet the inhabitants of the country are accustomed to grieve and weep at parting with the king's son. But if there is a wise man present, he says to them, Why do ye weep? Is it not the king's son? Is it not just that he should leave us and dwell in his father's palace? If all the just should know this, they would welcome the day when they must leave this earth. Is it not the height of glory that the queen, the (Scheinah, or the Divine Presence,) should come down in the midst of them, that they should be admitted to the king's palace, and should live in delight forevermore and enjoy everlasting happiness?"

In the following passage the Zohar shows that the world is full of spirits:

"God animated every particle of matter with a particular spirit. Forthwith, all the celestial armies were formed, and stood before him—with the breath of his mouth, he created all his armies. The spirits are the messengers of the Lord."

In order to show conclusively that the Cabalists, precisely like the believers in the Pitris in India, believed also in mediating, directing, and inspiring spirits, as well as in evil spirits, we propose to make one more quotation, which shall be the last, from the eminent translator and commentator to whom we have already so often referred.

"We shall understand still better," he says, "what is meant by the spirits animating all the celestial bodies, and all the elements of the earth, if we pay particular attention to the names and functions attributed to them. In the first place, we must dismiss from our minds all the purely poetical personifications, of whose character there is the slightest doubt. Such are all the angels which are named either after a moral quality or a metaphysical abstraction, such, for instance, as good and evil desires, which are represented as real persons, acting in our presence; Tahariel, the spirit of purity; Rachmiel, the spirit of mercy; Tsadkiel, the spirit of justice; Padael, the spirit of deliverance, and the famous Raziel, the spirit of secrecy, which watches with a jealous eye over the mysteries of Cabalistic wisdom. It is, moreover, a principle recognized by all Cabalists as a part of the general system of being that the angelic hierarchy only commences with the third world, which is called the World of Formation, or, as they say, in the space occupied by the planets and celestial bodies. The chief of these invisible forces is the angel Metratrone, so called because he stands immediately below the throne of God, and alone forms the World of Creation or of pure spirits. His task is to preserve unity, harmony, and motion in all the spheres. His office is precisely the same as that of that blind and indefinite power which it is sometimes proposed to substitute for God under the name of Nature. He has under his orders myriads of subjects, who are divided into ten categories, no doubt, in honor of the ten Zephiroth. These subordinate spirits maintain the same relation to the different parts of nature as their chief does to the universe. Thus, one presides over the movements of the earth, another over those of the moon, and the same is true of the other celestial bodies. One is called the spirit of fire, Nouriel; another the spirit of light, Ouriel; a third presides over the distribution of the seasons; a fourth, over vegetation. Finally, all productions, all the forces, and all the phenomena of nature are represented in the same way."

As for the evil spirits, which the Cabalists also believe in, they regard them as grosser and more imperfect forms of existence. In the darkness and impurity in which they move, they are divided, like the superior spirits, into ten categories, personifying evil in all its degrees.

It will be readily seen that upon all these points the Hindu Book of the Pitris and the Hebrew Zohar are inspired with the same idea. There is the same metaphysical basis, the same belief in good and bad spirits, and the same system with regard to the composition of the universe.

Although we are not in possession of any very precise information with regard to the *evocation of spirits* by the Cabalists, who probably never transmitted the prescribed formulas, except by word of mouth, still Hebraic tradition is so full to overflowing of the phenomena of evocation and occult manifestations, which are a necessary outgrowth of the beliefs we have just set forth, that it would be puerile to ask whether the ancient Cabalists, like the Hindu priests, ever claimed to exercise supernatural power.

We need only remind the reader of the witch of Endor, evoking the ghost of Samuel, the prophet, before Saul, on the eve of the battle of Gilboa; of Daniel explaining, in the presence of Balthazar, the magical writing upon the walls of his palace, *by an invisible hand*, in the midst of a feast:

Mene—Tekel—Upharsin;

and of the witch Huldah, whom the high priest Hilkiah made use of, in order to influence the people, as well as of hundreds of other similar facts which are clearly nothing but exterior manifestations of an occult power.

We may be told, however, in opposition, that the Jewish Cabala cannot lay claim to such antiquity. It is the unanimous opinion of all Cabalists that this mysterious philosophy sprang originally from the primitive institution of the Levites, and grew out of their desire to arrogate to themselves a belief of a higher order than that which they vulgarly taught.

We are indebted to Cabalistic tradition for the following legend, which we give in conclusion:[1]

"One day, our Master Jochanan Ben Zachai started upon his travels. He rode a donkey and was followed by Rabbi Eleazar Ben Aroch. The latter asked him to teach him a chapter of the Mercaba. 'Did not I tell you,' answered our master, 'that it was not lawful to explain the Mercaba unto one alone, if he did not possess the requisite degree of wisdom and intelligence?' 'Is it not lawful,' replied Eleazar, 'at any rate, for me to repeat in your presence what you have already taught me?' 'Well, speak,' said our master. Saying so, he dismounted, drew a veil over his head, and sat down upon a stone in the shadow of an olive tree. Eleazar, son of Aroch, had hardly commenced speaking of the Mercaba, when a fire descended from heaven and enveloped all the trees in the country, which seemed to sing hymns, and in the midst of the fire, *a spirit* was heard to express his joy at hearing these mysteries."

In the same passage we are told that two others who

[1] Thal. Bab. Traii. Chaguiga, fol. xiv.

had been initiated, Rabbi Josuah and Rabbi Joseph, following Eleazar's example, recited a chapter of the Mercaba. The most extraordinary prodigies again occurred.

"The sky was covered with thick clouds, a meteor very much like a rainbow appeared in the horizon, and the spirits were seen flocking to hear them, like spectators crowding to witness the passage of a wedding."

Upon learning of the prodigies which had been accomplished by his disciples Jochanan Ben Zachai told of one in his turn, which was as follows:

"We had been transported upon Mount Sinai, when from the heavens above a voice was heard, uttering these words: Come up here, where a splendid feast is provided for you, and for your disciples, and for all the generations who may hear these doctrines. You are destined to enter the third category."

Thus the phenomena of external manifestations, such as *the fire hovering around the trees*, and a *meteor suddenly exhibiting itself among the clouds*; the phenomena of evocation, such as *the spirits flocking to hear the mysterious secrets of the Mercaba*; the phenomena of transformation, where Jochanan and *his disciples were transported upon Mount Sinai to converse with the invisible spirits*; and finally, *their admission to the third category of initiation*, in short, everything in this Cabalistic passage, goes to show that those who believed in the Zohar claimed the power to *evoke spirits* and to produce external phenomena.

CHAPTER VIII.

POINTS OF RESEMBLANCE BETWEEN THE DOCTRINE OF THE PITRIS AND THAT OF THE ZEND-AVESTA OF PERSIA, THE PHILOSOPHY OF PLATO, THE ALEXANDRIAN SCHOOL, AND OF CHRISTIANITY.

The Jewish Cabala is not the only philosophical system in ancient times which closely resembles the Brahminical doctrine.

According to Plato, the universe was an emanation from the Supreme Being, created by the Word, or Son, and was a mere reproduction of the eternal types contained in the divine wisdom; like the Hindus he believes in the pre-existence of the soul, and metempsychosis, and like them he *secretly* instructed those who had been initiated in doctrines of which those he popularly taught gave but a faint idea.

If we may apply that expression to him, the philosopher of Egina was what we should call in modern times, an eclectic.

He taught his disciples, in a smaller compass, the traditions of human wisdom, which had been handed down from age to age to his time, by means of the mystic initiations in the temples.

We are positively told so by Proclus, in the following passage:

"Ἀπάσαν μὲν τοῦ Πλάτωνος φιλοσοφίαν, καὶ τὴν ἀρχὴν ἐκλάμψαι νομίζω, κατὰ τὴν τῶν κρειττόνων ἀγαθοειδῆ βουλῆσιν . . . τῆς τε ἄλλης ἀπάσης ἥμας μετόχοος κατέσ-

τησε τοῦ Πλάτωνος φιλοσοφίας, καὶ κοινωνοὺς τῶν ἐν ἀποῤῥήτοις παρὰ των αὐτου πρεσβυτέρων μετείληφε."

There are so many points of analogy between the philosophy of the Alexandrian school, or Neo-platonism, and the Hindu doctrines which we have just been investigating, that we cannot avoid the conclusion that the former was derived from that inexhaustible Oriental fountain. Moreover, it claims, itself, to have sprung from the mysterious traditions of Asia.

Its idea of God is that he is the Great All, from which everything proceeds, and to which everything tends.

He is all and everything is in him.

He is unity, *τὸ ἕν*;

He is the ineffable, *ἀῤῥητός*;

He is the unknown, *ἀγνωστός*.

According to Plotinus and his school, the Trinity is an emanation from unity, exactly as held by those who believe in the Pitris.

It receives the following names, taken from its attributes:

τὸ ἕν, το αγαθὸν, unity or, in other words, the good.

Νοῦς, the soul of the world, or the universal spirit.

Ψυχὴ τοῦ παντός, τῶν ὅλων, the demiourgos, or the creator.

The resemblance between the two systems is not confined, however, to a single point. Each member of this trinity begets, in its turn, a special trinity, and the mission of the three trinities that spring from them, is to produce unceasingly and to perpetuate in this world, first, the good; second, the intelligence or the vital principle; and third, the work of creation.

Under more mystical names they are precisely similar to the three trinities of the Brahmins and the Cabalists.

According to the Neo-platonists the Supreme Being,

with its various symbolic transformations, is a vast and everlasting source, from which are constantly springing those universal races which, through the love of the husband for his spouse, of the unity for the intelligence, are provided with all the different attributes and are thereby impelled to ascend unceasingly, through successive transformations, until they arrive at unity itself.

"By a movement like that of an endless chain about a wheel," as the Book of the Pitris says.

Between the Trinitarian systems of Christianity and those of the Hindus, of the Cabalists, and of the Neoplatonists, the numerous points of similarity are obvious at a glance, and we can readily see the source from which the founders of that religion have derived their revelation.

We say founders, though that is not the proper name to apply to the authors of the four gospels, whose idea it was to create a tradition of their own, for it is now well settled that Christianity, which is as old as the temples of Egypt and the pagodas of India, is a symbolic synthesis of all the beliefs of antiquity.

Scholars living in the primitive ages of the church were not so easily misled. In the third century, the illustrious Manichæan, Faustus, wrote these words, which we commend to the attention of all those who have made the life of Jesus the theme of romantic study:

"Everybody knows that the gospels were actually written neither by Jesus Christ nor by his personal disciples, but were carried along by tradition, and long after their time were written by unknown people, who, correctly supposing that their word would not be taken as to things that had not come under their personal observation, placed at the head of these traditional statements the names of the apostles or of apostolic men contemporaneous with them." (Faustus.)

The Council of Nice, under the presidency of Constantine, that odious and criminal despot, whose praises have been sung by all the writers of the Church, indeed created a Catholicism, as a means of discipline, which was entirely different from primitive Christianity.

In very guarded language, Franck expresses a similar opinion in the following words:

"Have we not every reason in the world to look upon the Cabala as a precious relic *of the religious philosophy of the East*, which was transported to Alexandria and became mingled with the teachings of Plato, and whose influence—under cover of the usurped name of Denys, the Areopagite—Bishop of Athens, who was converted and consecrated by Saint Paul—was felt in the mysticism of the middle ages?"

To the question, What is, then, this religious philosophy of the East, whose influence is apparent in the mystic symbols of Christianity? we answer as follows:

The philosophy, of which we find traces among the Magi, the Chaldeans, the Egyptians, the Hebrew Cabalists, and the Christians, is identical with that of the Hindu Brahmins, who believed in the Pitris.

There is one argument in favor of this opinion which is absolutively conclusive, and that is this: Among all ancient countries, India is the only one that possesses the whole of this philosophy, so much so, indeed, that if it were desired to reconstruct it from materials obtained from other sources than the immortal thinkers of the banks of the Ganges, it would be necessary to borrow them at second hand, here and there, from the various quarters wherever found, from Plato, from the Cabala, from the Alexandrian school, from the Magi, and from Christianity.

On the other hand, the high antiquity of the mighty work performed in India is opposed to the supposition, even for an instant, that the Brahminical philosophy was formed of pieces and fragments taken from these different systems, which, being posterior to the Vedas and Manu—that nobody disputes—were not, as admitted even by those who hold most firmly to the opposite view, born upon the soil where we now find them.

If the Cabala, if Magism, Plato, the Alexandrian school, and Christianity did not derive their doctrines from original sources, if, on the contrary, we find them in the remotest ages in the philosophical works of ancient India, not as isolated facts but as a complete collection of beliefs, dogmas, and mysteries, which go to make up the whole of what is called the Brahminic civilization, have we not every reason to maintain that they came originally from the country of the Vedas?

It is easy to trace through the ages the path of these lofty speculations. From India they made their way into Persia and Chaldea, both by means of emigration and natural infiltration. It is sufficient to compare the traditions of the Boun-Dehesh and the Zend-Avesta with those that have been the object of our study, in order to recognize their similarity, only the system of the Parsees and of the ancient Chaldeans is less philosophical than that of the mother country, and concedes to the *dews* and evil spirits a much greater degree of importance than that which is recognized by the Indian theory, as possessed by the Devas and Pisatchas.

We shall have to descend to the superstitious of vulgar Brahminism, we shall have to go to the religion of the Soudra, in order to find a like severity of conflict between the spirits of good and the spirits of evil. Parseeism and Chaldeaism are a mixture of the gross superstitions of the Hindu populace and of the philosophical conceptions of the Brahmins.

This reminds us of the following lines, which we quote from Amniance Marcellinus and which are confirmed by Agathias.

"The King Hytaspes, having penetrated as far as certain retired places *in Upper India*, came to some solitary groves, whose silence seem to be favorable *to the profound thoughts of the Brahmins.* There they taught him, as far as they possibly could, the pure sacrificial rites, and the causes of the movement of the stars and the universe, a part of which he communicated to the Magi. The latter have transmitted these secrets from father to son, together with the science of predicting the future. Since then, during a long succession of ages until now, there have arisen a multitude of Magi, belonging to the same race, who have devoted themselves to the service of the temple and the worship of the Gods."

Egypt, which had never forgotten its early traditions, was constantly drawing new life and vigor from the study of the scientific movement of Upper Asia.

Moses of Chorenus, who lived five centuries before the present era, bears witness to this, in the most positive manner, in the following passage:

"The ancient Asiatics had a multitude of historical works which were translated into Greek, when the Ptolemies established the Alexandrian library and encouraged literary men by their liberality, so that the Greek language became the depositary of all the ancient learning."

It is evident from all this, first, that people in ancient times did not live a more isolated life from each other, as regards the philosophical and religious sciences, than they do now. Second, that there was a large collection of traditions, of which ancient India was the principal source. Third, that a close connection existed between the teachings of the Brahmins and the systems of the Magi, the Chaldeans, the Cabalists, the Platonists, and the philosophers of the Alexandrian School, whose sect called therapeutæ kept alive the traditions which afterward became those of Christianity.

By the careful study and comparison of the old civilizations we thus acquire a knowledge of the general drift and tendency of the human intellect in those times, without regard to the warring claims of rival sects or the conflicting pretensions of individual pride.

There is not a fact, not a belief, not a discovery, that is independent of tradition, and those who, in order to display their singularity and to make a particular place for their special studies, are constantly meeting with conceptions which lay claim to originality and are said to have borrowed nothing from any that have preceded them, are unmindful of the laws of history and of the evolution of the human mind.

FOURTH PART.

EXOTERIC MANIFESTATIONS AND DEMONSTRATIONS AMONG THE INITIATES OF THE SACRED TEMPLES OF INDIA, AS SHOWN BY THE PERFORMING FAKIRS.

Power belongs to him who knows. (Agrouchada-Parikchai.)

He who has penetrated the secret of things, who has lifted himself up by contemplation to the knowledge of the immortal principle, who has mortified his body and developed his soul, who knows all the mysteries of being and not being, who has studied all the transformations of the vital molecule from Brahma to man and from man to Brahma, he alone is in communication with the Pitris and commands the celestial forces. (Atharva-Veda.)

The Boutams (or bad spirits) tremble before him who is shaved, who wears the triple girdle, and is clothed with the yellow vestment, and who carries the seven-knotted stick. (Agrouchada-Parikchai.)

TO THE READER.

The philosophical part of our work is now ended. In a subject so vast there are many points, no doubt, that might have been more fully developed, but our main purpose has been to give a comprehensive idea of the metaphysical speculations of the Hindu initiates, and to show that their belief in spirits was only a consequence of their system relating to God and his attributes, and to the existence of the universe. In the comparison of this doctrine, which is based upon the Vedas themselves, with those of other ancient people, we devoted most of the space at our command to the Jewish Cabala, because, though not so well known as Magism, the philosophy of Plato, or the Alexandrian school, it also believed in the manifestations of spirits, the power of evocation, and its external phenomena, precisely in the same manner as the philosophy of the Pitris, their traditional ancestor on the banks of the Ganges.

We might also have called attention to the fact that primitive Christianity, with its Thaumaturgists suddenly appearing through closed doors, raising the dead, floating in the air, and receiving the gift of tongues, with its initiation in the Catacombs, its superior spirits, its demons, and its exorcists, was intimately related to the Cabala and the doctrine of the Pitris. We confined ourselves, however, to the statement that that religious revolution in the earlier ages of our era was only a synthesis of the old beliefs of Asia. An exhaustive study of the subject would have required a book by itself, which we might not have the leisure to complete.

The special scope of the present work forbids any extended excursion into this field. The mere fact of our undertaking it would have necessarily led us to devote the same space to the mysterious initiations of Egpyt, Chaldea, and Persia, and, as the reader will readily see, it would have compelled us to write a general history of the ancient civilizations of the East, such as forms a part of the ethnographical studies published by us elsewhere.

Before giving an account of the exterior phenomena and manifestations by which the Hindus claim to show that they are in possession of occult power, which is a logical consequence of their religious belief in the part played by spirits in the universe, we desire to disavow any personal responsibility whatever.

We assert nothing positively with regard to most of the facts which we are about to relate. The skill derived from long experience, charlatanism, and even hallucination itself, may assist to explain them. We are bound to say, however, as impartial and faithful observers, that though we applied the severest tests, to which the Fakirs and other initiates interposed no objection whatever, we never succeeded in detecting a single case of fraud or trickery, which, we admit, is far from being a conclusive proof of their honesty.

Huc, the missionary, who also gives an account of similar phenomena, witnessed by him in Thibet, was equally at a loss to account for them.

We are perfectly ready to admit, also, that we never knew a European, either in India or Ceylon, even among the oldest residents, who was able to indicate what means the votaries of the Pitris used in the production of these phenomena.

Is this tantamount to saying that we believe in the intervention of invisible spirits?

We do not believe in spiritualism, but while we believe that *scepticism or doubt in all cases*, in spite of any amount of proof, is something that man, in his weakness, has no right to indulge in, we may add, on the other hand, that no one has a right to assert a thing positively or scientifically, except upon careful investigation, based upon proof upon either side.

We occupy the position which we assumed in our preface, viz.: That of a simple recorder of facts which some regard as occult manifestations and others as skilful jugglery.

There are, however, some phenomena, which, without going too far, we are inclined to attribute to natural forces, the laws of which have not yet been ascertained.

What are these forces? Or rather, what is the force which the Hindus attribute to the pure Agasa fluid, under the direction of the spirits?

We are not an authority upon this point, and when we see the illustrious scientist and member of the Royal Society of London, William Crookes, treated with ridicule and contempt on account of the inquiries he is now making with a view to the discovery of the laws of this force, we are involuntarily reminded of the words of *Galvani*, to whom the western world is indebted for the earliest experiments in electricity, as follows:

"I am attacked by two classes of persons, the learned and the ignorant. Both of them treat me with ridicule, and say that I am only fit to be *a dancing-master for frogs*,[1] and yet I think that I have discovered one of the grandest forces in nature."

In short, with regard to certain physical facts, which have nothing in common with supernatural evocations, apparitions, or manifestations, and which are not in direct opposition to the laws of nature, which are not more wonderful than the results produced by electricity, we think that a denial or affirmation following a thorough

[1] Alluding to his experiments on frogs.

and scientific investigation, is better than a denial or affirmation *à priori*.

We know what a denial *à priori* is worth. It once rejected steam and electricity.

The phenomena which we shall describe are all included within the three following categories:

First, facts and phenomena of exterior manifestations, obtained by spiritual force, and generally with the aid of material objects.

Second, facts of a magnetic or somnambulistic character.

Third, the phenomena of evocation and apparition, and the production of material objects by the spirits.

Phenomena of the first class are apparently easily tested. We shall tell what we have done and what our experience has been, without, however, expressing any opinion of our own as to their causes.

As to the last class of cases, we should have omitted them altogether from the present work, as shunning a scientific investigation, if—remembering that in ancient times the belief in evocations and apparitions was universal; that all religions, with Christianity at their head, included such phenomena in their mysteries and miracles—we had not deemed that it would be at least a matter of historical curiosity to set forth the nature of these singular practices—in common use in India at the present day—which are so well adapted to influence the popular mind, and which formed the basis of all the ancient superstitions.

CHAPTER I.

AS TO WHO ARE INITIATED INTO THE DIFFERENT CLASSES OF OCCULT POWER.

We have already seen what a long life of prayer, maceration, ablution, and fasting the novices were required to pass in the different degrees of initiation. We now dismiss that branch of our subject.

It may not be amiss, however, to remind the reader that the initiated possessed powers, more or less extensive, according to the class to which they belonged, and to indicate the nature of these powers.

The first class comprised:

First.—The Grihastas.

Second.—The Pourohitas.

Third.—The Fakirs.

The Grihastas or heads of families do not forsake the world. They are a sort of connecting link between the temple and the people. They are formally forbidden to make any manifestations of external phenomena. It is their right, however, and their duty to evoke the souls of their ancestors, in some retired part of their dwelling, and to receive from them, as their direct descendants, only such instruction as they need for their guidance in this earthly pilgrimage.

The Pourohitas, or priests of the popular cult, take part in all family ceremonies. They evoke familiar spirits and drive away evil spirits. They cast horoscopes and preside over births, marriages, and funerals. They perform all the phenomena of auspicious or inauspicious omens and intervene in all cases of over-excitement or possession, to remove from the subject all malign influences. They confine themselves strictly to the domain of religion.

The performing Fakirs collect alms and money in the temples, and wander over the country and through the cities. They produce at will the strangest phenomena, entirely contrary to what are conventionally called natural laws. With the aid of spirits, who are present at all their operations, as claimed by the Brahmins, they have authority, as well as power, to evoke them.

The second class includes:

THE SANNYASSIS.

The third class includes:

First.—THE NIRVANYS.

Second.—THE YOGUYS.

In these two higher grades of initiation the power is the same, only differing in degree. They claim to have subjected the visible as well as the invisible world to their will, and only produce their supernatural manifestations in the interior of the temples and, in very rare cases, before the Rajahs or other eminent personages in India.

According to their account, time, space, specific gravity, and even life itself, are nothing to them. They enjoy the faculty of laying aside, or resuming, their mortal envelope. They command the elements, transport mountains, and drain rivers. Upon this point the Oriental imagination, which knows no limits, gives itself the fullest scope, and these spiritual lights are regarded in India as gods.

There is here presented, as we see, a complete organization resting upon the caste system, and adapted to the support of a social state, entirely sacerdotal.

It is claimed that these different initiates undergo, during a period of many years, in the subterranean sanctuaries of the pagodas, a course of training, which modifies their organization, from a physiological point of view, and increases to a large extent the production of the pure fluid emanating from them, called agasa. It is impossible for us to obtain any authentic information concerning these occult practices.

It is mainly with reference to the Fakirs that we propose to investigate these different phenomena.

CHAPTER II.

AGASA.

In order to make ourselves understood, where there is as yet no accepted mode of speech, we will say what we mean by the term "spirit force."

By "spirit force" we mean the alliance between the intellect and the physical forces, in order to act upon inanimate objects, without pre-determining, in any way, the cause which sets this force in motion.

The meaning of the word is not strictly, perhaps, that which is generally attached to it. We will therefore say that we use it only to classify the phenomena which we are about to describe, and that the meaning here given expresses accurately the signification of the term used by the Hindus.

The supreme cause of all phenomena, according to the Brahmins, is the pure agasa fluid, or the vital fluid, which is diffused throughout nature, and puts animate or inanimate, visible or invisible beings, in communication with each other. Heat, electricity, all the forces of nature, in short, are but modes of action and particular states of this fluid.

The being who possesses an excess of this vital fluid acquires a proportionate power, both over animate beings not so highly favored, and over inanimate beings. The spirits themselves are sensible to the influence of this universal fluid, and can place their power at the service of those who are able to evoke them.

According to some Brahmins, agasa is the moving thought of the universal soul, directing all souls, who would be in constant communication with each other, if the gross envelope of the body did not in a measure prevent. Thus, the more completely the soul disentangles itself from its vestment—the body—by contemplation, the more sensible it becomes to this universal fluid, whereby all beings, whether visible or invisible, are united.

Such is the theory. We merely set it forth and propose to confine ourselves to the rôle of an interpreter and nothing more.

CHAPTER III.

THE PERFORMING FAKIRS.

EVERY European has heard of the extraordinary skill of the Hindu Fakirs, who are popularly designated under the name of Charmers or Jugglers. They claim to be invested with supernatural powers. Such is the belief of all Asiatic people.

When our countrymen are told of their performances, they usually answer: go to the regular magicians, they will show you the same things.

To enable the reader to appreciate the grounds of this opinion, it seems necessary to show how the Fakirs operate. The following are facts which no traveller has ventured to contradict.

First.—They never give public representations in places where the presence of several hundred persons makes it impossible to exercise the proper scrutiny.

Second.—They are accompanied by no assistant or confederate, as they are usually termed.

Third.—They present themselves in the interior of the house completely naked, except that they wear, for modesty's sake, a small piece of linen about as large as the hand.

Fourth.—They are not acquainted with goblets, or magic bags, or double-bottomed boxes, or prepared tables, or any of the thousand and one things which our European conjurors find necessary.

Fifth.—They have absolutely nothing in their possession, save a small wand of seven knots of young bamboo, as big as the handle of a pen-holder, which they hold in their right hand, and a small whistle, about three inches long, which they fasten to one of the locks of their long, straight hair; for, having no clothes and consequently no pockets, they would otherwise be obliged to hold it constantly in their hands.

Sixth.—They operate, as desired by the person whom they are visiting, either in a sitting or standing posture or, as the case may require, upon the marble, granite, or stucco pavement of the veranda, or upon the bare ground in the garden.

Seventh.—When they need a subject for the exhibition of magnetic or somnambulistic phenomena, they take any of your servants whom you may designate, no matter whom, and they act with the same facility upon a European, in case he is willing to serve.

Eighth.—If they need any article, such as a musical instrument, a cane, a piece of paper, a pencil, etc., they ask you to furnish it.

Ninth.—They will repeat any experiments in your presence as many times as you require, and will submit to any test you may apply.

Tenth.—They never ask any pay, merely accepting as alms for the temple to which they are attached, whatever you choose to offer them.

I have travelled through India in every direction for many years, and I can truthfully state that I have never seen a single Fakir who was not willing to comply with any of these conditions.

It only remains for us to ask, whether our more popular magicians would ever consent to dispense with any of their numerous accompaniments and perform under the same conditions.

There is no doubt what the answer would be.

Without drawing any conclusions as to causes or methods, I merely state the facts.

CHAPTER IV.

THE LEAF DANCE.

We select at random some facts that fell under our own observation, as they were noted down at the time, grouping them, however, according to the method adopted by us, to make the Hindu classification more clear.

What we call spirit force is called by the Hindus arta-ahancârasya or the force of I.

I had been a resident of Pondichéry, the capital of the French possessions in the Carnatic, for several years, when one morning, between eleven and twelve o'clock, my do-bachy or valet-de-chambre informed me that a Fakir wanted to see me.

I had left Europe without the slightest idea of the phenomena which the spiritualists attribute to their mediums. I was ignorant of the very principles lying at the bottom of a faith which I then believed to be new, but which I now know to be as old as the temples of India, Chaldea, and Egypt for all religions commenced with the belief in spirits and outward manifestations, the source of a revelation claimed to be divine. I had not even seen a single case of table-tipping. The extravagances of the faith in invisible spirits in which its adepts sincerely believed, and which always formed a prominent feature of their stories, were so like the ecstasies, the mysterious apparitions, and the whole machinery of the Catholic church, that it had never occurred to me, ardent naturalist as I was, to attend or witness one of the experiments which had stirred up such a general interest in every direction.

As for the Hindu Fakirs, I conceived them to be simple magicians, and I unceremoniously dismissed them whenever they presented themselves. Yet I had heard a great deal of their marvellous skill, and I was anxious to see a specimen of it.

The Hindu having been admitted, I received him in one of the interior verandas of my house. I was struck first by his extreme leanness; his face was as thin and bony as that of an anchorite, and his eyes, which seemed half dead, produced a sensation such as I once experienced when looking at the motionless, green orbs of a large deep-water shark.

He was waiting for me in a squatting posture upon the marble floor; when he saw me he arose slowly. Bowing with his hands raised to his forehead, he murmured the following:

"Saranai aya" (I greet you respectfully, Sahib), "it is I, Salvanadin-Odéar, son of Canagarayen-Odéar. May the immortals watch over your days."

"Salam, Salvanadin-Odéar, son of Canagarayen-Odéar, may you die upon the sacred banks of the Tircangey, and may that transformation be your last."

"The guru of the pagoda said to me this morning," continued the Hindu, "go and glean at random, like the birds in the rice-fields, and Ganésa, the god of travellers, has led me to your house."

"You are welcome."

"What do you want of me?"

"You are said to possess the faculty of communicating movement to inert bodies without touching them. I should like to see a specimen of your power."

"Salvanadin-Odéar has no such power; he merely evokes spirits, who lend him their aid."

"Well, let Salvanadin-Odéar evoke the spirits, and show me what they can do."

The words were hardly out of my mouth when the Fakir resumed his squatting position upon the pavement, placing his seven-knotted stick between his crossed legs.

He then asked to have my dobachy bring seven small flower-pots full of earth, seven thin sticks of wood each about two cubits long, and seven leaves taken from any tree, no matter what.

When these different articles had been brought, without touching them himself, he had them placed in a horizontal line, about two yards from his outstretched arm. He instructed my servant to plant a stick of wood in each pot of earth, and to put on each stick a tree leaf with a hole in the middle.

This being done, all the leaves dropped down the sticks, acting as covers to the pots. The Fakir then joined his hands and raised them above his head, and I heard him distinctly utter, in the Tamoul language, the following invocation:

"May all the powers that watch over the intellectual principle of life (kche'tradjna) and over the principle of matter (boûtatoma) protect me from the wrath of the pisatchas (evil spirits), and may the immortal spirit, which has three forms (mahatatridandi, the trinity), shield me from the vengeance of Yama."

At the close of the invocation he stretched out his hands in the direction of the flower-pots, and stood motionless, in a sort of ecstasy. From time to time his lips moved as if he were continuing his occult invocation, but no sound reached my ears.

I watched all these elaborate preparations with considerable interest and amusement, without suspecting what was to follow. Suddenly it seemed to me that my hair was moved by a slight current of air, which blew in my face like one of those gusts that we often see in the tropics after sunset, and yet the large straw curtains of vétivert, hanging in the vacant spaces between the columns of the veranda, were undisturbed. I thought that my senses had deceived me, but the phenomenon was repeated several times.

At the end of about a quarter of an hour, though there

had been no change of position on the part of the Fakir, the fig-leaves began to move slowly upward along the sticks of wood, and then as slowly descend.

I approached and watched them as they continued their motion with the closest attention. I must confess that when I saw that there was no visible means of communication between the Hindu and the leaves I was very much surprised.

I passed and repassed several times in the space which separated the juggler from the pots of earth, but there was no interruption in the ascent or descent of the leaves.

I asked to examine his arrangements and was unhesitatingly allowed to do so. I removed the leaves from the sticks, and the sticks from the pots, and emptied their contents upon the pavement. Having rung for the *cousicara* (or cook) I ordered seven goblets to be brought from the kitchen, and some earth and fresh leaves from the garden. I divided the bamboo stick myself into seven pieces, and I arranged everything as it had been done previously, placing it all at about four yards from the Fakir, who looked on unconcernedly during the whole operation, without making any remark or movement whatever.

"Do you think," I then asked him, "that the spirits will act now?"

He made no answer, but merely extended his arms, as he had done before.

Five minutes had hardly elapsed, when the upward and downward motion of the leaves along the sticks was repeated.

I was amazed and it must be confessed that I had ample reason.

Still I would not acknowledge my defeat. I asked the Fakir if the pots of earth were essential to the production of the phenomena, and, being answered in the negative, I had seven holes bored in a plank, in which I placed the bamboo sticks. In a short time, the same phenomena occurred as before.

During the next two hours, I repeated the experiment in twenty different ways, but always with the same result.

The only way in which I could account for it was by supposing that I was under some powerful magnetic influence. The Fakir said to me: "Is there not some question you wish to put to the invisible spirits before they go?"

The question was totally unexpected, but as I had heard that European mediums use an alphabet in conversing with spirits, as they claim, I explained the matter to the Hindu, and asked him if I could enter into communication with them by any such means.

He answered me in these words, "Ask anything you please, the leaves will remain still, if the spirits have nothing to say. If, on the contrary, those who guide them have any communication to make, they will move upward along the sticks."

I was about to write an alphabet upon a sheet of paper when a very simple device occurred to me. I had a set of raised brass letters and figures upon zinc blocks which I used to stamp my name and a number upon the books in my library. I threw them pell-mell into a small linen bag, and the Fakir having resumed his position of invocation, I thought of a friend, who had died twenty years before, and proceeded to extract the letters and numbers, one by one.

Upon taking up each of the zinc blocks I looked at the letter or figure as I called it off, and kept a watchful eye upon the leaves so that the least movement would not escape me.

I had already taken out fourteen blocks and nothing unusual had occurred, when upon the appearance of the letter A, the leaves began to move, and after ascending to the top of the sticks, fell again to the boards in which the pieces of bamboo had been placed.

I could not help betraying some emotion, when I observed that the motion of the leaves corresponded to the appearance of the first letter of my friend's name.

When the bag was empty, I put the letters and figures in again, and continued as before. Letter by letter and figure by figure I obtained the following words:

Albain Brunier, died at Bourg-en-bresse (Ain) January 3, 1856.

The name, the date, the place, everything was correct; the blood rushed to my head as I read over and over again, the words which shone strangely in my eyes.

What made my astonishment still greater was the fact that I had no conception of phenomena of this class. I was totally unprepared for them; I wanted to be alone and to reflect. I therefore dismissed the Fakir, without making any further observations on that day. I made him promise, however, to come on the morrow, at the same hour.

He was punctual to the appointment.

We repeated the same series of experiments, and the result was the same as before.

The excitement which I had at first experienced, and which was perfectly natural under the circumstances, had disappeared, but I was no nearer than before to a belief in the supernatural and in the reality of the Fakir's evocations. I was merely led to formulate in my own mind the following supposition:

"If these phenomena were not the result of pure charlatanism, magnetic influence, or hallucination, perhaps there is a natural force, the laws of which we are yet ignorant of, and which enables its possessor to act upon inanimate objects, and interpret thoughts, as the telegraph puts two minds in communication in different and opposite parts of the globe."

I spent a portion of the night in reflection upon this point. On the morrow I repeated the phenomena of the previous day at an early sitting. I then asked the Fakir to do them over again, and I watched them, having in mind the supposition aboved named.

When I asked the Fakir, for instance, to repeat the communication of the previous day, I changed in my mind the orthography of the name, dwelling strongly upon each letter. The following variations were the result:

Halbin Pruniet, died, etc.

I may add, however, that when I tried to change the name of the city, or of the date of the occurrence, I was unsuccessful at that time and that the message was always the same and always correct in those respects:

Died at Bourg-en-Bresse (Ain) *January* 3, 1856.

During fifteen days I had the Fakir at my house every day, and he always submitted, with the utmost readiness, to all my requirements. I varied my experiments as follows:

Bearing in mind always the exact words of the message as I first received it, I wanted to know positively, whether it was possible to effect a complete change in its terms.

At one time I obtained changes in the letters composing the name, so that no one would have recognized it; at another time, the changes referred to the date of the day, of the month, or of the year, but I never obtained the slightest alteration in the name of the city, which was invariably the same:

Bourg-en-Bresse.

Hence I concluded—referring always to the supposition under which I was acting, that there really was a natural force, which had established a communication between myself and the Fakir and the leaves—that I could not sufficiently isolate my mind from the correct orthography of all the words in the sentence.

On several different occasions I made similar attempts, with different subjects, but with no better result.

While, on the one hand, the material phenomena were repeated with scarcely any variation to speak of, still, there were constant changes in the interpretation of my thoughts, which were sometimes designed on my part, and sometimes, on the contrary, in direct opposition to what I had intended. In the last sitting the Fakir gave, he lowered one balance of a pair of scales simply with a peacock's feather, when the other balance contained a weight of about a hundred and seventy pounds. By the mere imposition of hands, he made a crown of flowers float in the the air, the atmosphere was filled with vague and indistinct sounds and a shadowy hand drew luminous figures in space. At that time I considered the two latter phenomena simply as phantasmagoria—I did not even give them the benefit of a doubt. For this reason, my notes of this sitting do not contain a full and accurate account of the facts. I shall describe them farther on with suitable details in the case of other magicians by whom they were also performed.

In short, with regard to purely material facts, I may say that I never detected the slightest deception, and I applied the severest tests in order to discover any fraud.

As for physiological facts, dismissing the hypothesis of supernatural intervention, and on the simple supposition of a spiritual communication between the operator and his assistant, I am bound to say that I personally obtained nothing fixed, nothing invariable.

Such were my first observations at Pondichéry. My judicial duties and special studies concerning ancient India did not give me time to continue them, particularly in view of the results obtained, which were positive enough with regard to all material phenomena, it is true, but were doubtful and uncertain with regard to the transmission of mental messages between two persons in full possession of their faculties, but claimed to be in spiritual communication.

Perhaps there were grounds that might have warranted a further investigation into this material force, and, supposing that it really existed, for attempting to free it from the elaborate appliances and clap-trap by which it was encompassed, in order to strike the popular imagination. It was not, however, my business to do so, being otherwise occupied, as I have already said, by my professional duties and studies in relation to primitive society in Asia.

Still, while I took no further active interest in these phenomena, I was in the habit of setting apart anything I might meet with, in the course of my studies, relating to the doctrine of the Pitris, with the idea of publishing subsequently whatever I might come across upon a subject which seems to interest the Western, as much as it does the Asiatic world.

From this time forward I also made notes of all the material phenomena by whose aid the Fakirs seek to prove the existence of the power they claim, for it seems to me that such facts were strongly corroborative of their theory.

Although I have been careful to avoid any departure from the part which I have assumed as a simple historian, I have desired, in the present chapter, to give an account of the only attempts I have ever seriously made to inform myself regarding this force which the Fakirs appear to possess and by means of which, they claim, they hold communication with invisible spirits, a claim which many persons of our time, even of the highest intelligence, are disposed to allow. It seems to me that a reply is due to the reader who may ask: Why does the author disavow any personal responsibility? has he no opinion whatever upon this question?

I have indeed no *scientific opinion* upon this subject, as yet.

I am convinced that there are in nature, and in man, who is a part of nature, immense forces, the laws of which are yet unknown to us.

I think that man will some day discover these laws, that things that we now regard as dreams, will appear to us, in the future, as realities, and that we shall one day witness phenomena of which we have now no conception.

In the world of ideas, as in the material world, there is a period of gestation, as of birth. Who knows whether this psychic force, as the English call it—this force of the Ego, according to the Hindus, which the humble Fakir exhibited in my presence, will not be shown to be one of the grandest forces in nature?

I may be told that for more than ten thousand years, during which the Hindus have given it their attention, they have never succeeded in formulating the laws of this pretended force, and that we cannot afford to lose our time, now or in the future, as they have done.

The Brahmins have made everything subordinate to their religion, and we know that in *religious matters* there are no scientific experiments or proof. See what the middle ages produced in the domain of the exact sciences by taking their axioms from the words of the Bible!

From the remotest antiquity the pundits of the pagodas have been in the habit of bursting vessels by the use of compressed steam. They have also observed many electrical phenomena, but that has not led to the construction of railroads or telegraphs. Among ourselves, have we not seen scientific societies of the highest order officially treat Fulton like a crazy man, and regard the telegraph as a toy, only fit for sending messages from one room to another in the same dwelling. In the open air, and with atmospheric disturbances, the telegraph wire was not to be relied upon.

It has now, however, put a girdle round the earth, and we have sunk it at the bottom of the deepest seas.

See what human society as a whole has done. Every age turns an idea over and over again in all its phases; scientific men develop it and set forth their theory, from which they refuse to swerve; every scientific body has an opinion, to which it stoutly clings. If it does not say in so many words, "Thus far shalt thou go and no farther," everybody knows that it thinks so, for it rejects every idea that does not originate in its own bosom, everything new and startling. Then the new generation comes upon the stage and the sons rebel against their fathers, as behind the time. The screw traverses the ocean, regardless of wind or tide, and the electric fluid transmits thought to the four corners of the globe.

As I have been led to speak of my own views I will say that the conclusion that I have drawn from what I have seen in India, laying aside the clap-trap by which it is surrounded, and of which the Hindus are very fond, is that there is in man a special force acting in an unknown direction, and often intelligently, the laws of which require to be studied by unprejudiced and liberal-minded specialists.

Perhaps it is this force, developed by education and by a certain system of training, that the priests in the ancient temples set in motion, in order to impress the popular imagination by pretended prodigies.

In that case there would seem to be some foundation for the ancient stories and there probably was a real development of a natural force, in connection with an exhibition of the grossest superstition, moving the tree leaves at a distance, as well as the floral garlands and tapestry hung in the temples, adding several pounds to the weight of peacock's feathers, and producing musical sounds by the aid of concealed instruments.

It is to be hoped that our scientists will some day or other make a serious investigation into the production of some of these phenomena, which I saw repeated before my eyes, and which left no room for the slightest suspicion of charlatanism. I do not know that such is their intention, but it would be of some use, at any rate, whether it results in the exposure of a fraud, or whether it ends in the discovery of a new force in nature.

* * *

As I was putting in order for the press the different portions of this volume, which was written at Pondichéry in 1866, and which had slumbered in my drawer until then, for special reasons, I intended at first to omit that part of the present chapter where, departing from my rôle as a simple observer, I seemed to take sides in favor of a force, purely natural, it is true, but which produced phenomena that were apparently supernatural.

So far, I had rigidly excluded my personal opinions; should I now depart from this rule in that part of my book which treated of the more or less fantastical practices of the Hindus?

On the other hand, should I hesitate to acknowledge what seemed to be the few probably real facts, apart from the supernatural, which seemed to me to result from what I had seen?

I had not yet come to a decision on this point when, through the politeness of Dr. Puel, I was made acquainted with an article upon the psychic force, published by William Crookes, the eminent scientist and member of the Royal Society of London, in the *Quarterly Journal of Science,* one of the most respectable scientific organs of England.

I was not in England when the article appeared, and distance and my other studies made it impracticable for me to keep up my familiarity with works of this nature.

Imagine my surprise to see that the eminent chemist and physiologist had arrived at the positive conclusion, as the result of experiments similar to those I had seen in

India, that there exists a new force in the human organism, as I had timidly suggested, several years before, as a matter of supposition.

I immediately came to the determination to leave my chapter as I had written it, but to refer the reader to the article in question, as confirmatory of the position I had assumed.

If, in spite of all the precautions I have taken to banish anything in favor of a belief in the supernatural and to express my own opinion in the most hypothetical manner, I have laid myself open to the reproach of being too credulous, I shall bear the blame cheerfully, in the company of one of the most distinguished of English scientists.

* * * * * *

It appears that this force, which first suggested itself to my mind in 1866, in order to explain the phenomena which were then taking place in India before my face and eyes (the hypothesis that it was supernatural being totally inadmissible), had recently been recognized by physicians, astronomers, naturalists, and others, members of the Royal Society of London—which contains all who are eminent for their learning in England, as our Academy of Sciences contains men who are known and esteemed for their labors the world over—not, as I had done, by suggesting it as an hypothesis to explain certain phenomena, but by maintaining, after two years of experiments:

First, that there exists a force capable of moving heavy bodies without material contact, which depends in some unknown manner upon the presence of human beings.

Second, that nothing certain was known with regard to the nature and source of this force, but there is conclusive evidence that it exists.

Third, that movements can be produced in solid bodies without material contact by this hitherto unknown force, acting at an indefinite distance from the human organism, and wholly independent of muscular action.

Fourth, that this force makes solid bodies, which have no contact or visible or material connection with the bodies of any persons present, emit sounds which are distinctly heard by all present, and it is proved that these sounds proceed from these objects, by vibrations which are perfectly perceptible to the touch.

Fifth, that this force is frequently directed with intelligence.

The question is whether this is the force which the Hindus, who have known of its existence for thousands of years, have sought to develop in all subjects who were willing to become their tools, and who have afterward, with a view to religious domination, attributed its manifestations to superior spirits. We rather incline to think so, though we express no opinion as to its nature or origin. It is not with a view to elucidate this question, by showing what arguments may be urged on either hand, that we have given this brief sketch of what has been accomplished by English scientists upon this point. Our intention was simply to show that *scientific men* in England have officially recognized *the existence of a force, independent of muscular action, capable of moving bodies, of sometimes emitting melodious sounds, and which is frequently directed with intelligence*, and to draw the conclusion, from the similarity of the phenomena witnessed in England and in India, that the laws which govern them, in either country, are identical.

If some of the facts observed in India seem to be more wonderful than any which have formed the subject of experiment in England (I speak of the latter more particularly on account of the scientific endorsement they have received), the two following reasons may be given:

It is very possible that the Hindus, in addition to the real *force* they possess, also display a skill so great that it is difficult to detect them in any act of deception.

Perhaps, too, as they have been in possession, for several

thousand years, of this *special force*, they have discovered the laws which the *Englishmen* were unable to formulate, though they had proved the existence of the *force itself*.

It would follow therefrom that the discovery of the laws in question may have led to a more marked and decided progress in the production of these phenomena.

With these remarks, and without guaranteeing their *scientific value*, we will continue our account of the extraordinary manifestations which the Brahmins attribute to superior spirits, and which they hold to be a part of their religion.

We shall continue also, however, to indicate the efforts made by us to test them, as far as we were able. The accounts, as we have said before, are taken from our notes of travel in upper Bengal and the Himalaya Valleys. We have only omitted the descriptive portions and such facts as are of no general importance, being wholly personal.

CHAPTER V.

THE BRONZE VASE—MUSICAL ACCOMPANIMENTS.

"In view of the strange phenomena which succeed each other so rapidly, and which are as yet unexplained," says the learned Mr. Crookes, in the article to which we have referred, "I confess that it is difficult to avoid speaking of them in language of a somewhat sensational character."

While the incomparable light of a tropic sun and the splendors of Indian scenery form a natural and appropriate setting for these phenomena, and heighten their effect, they make it more difficult, however, for us to avoid the mistake pointed out by the eminent chemist of the Royal Society of London. Still, we think that it is possible to select words that shall express facts without making them more marvellous than they really are, and that shall simply and accurately describe the phenomena as they actually occurred.

We made no attempt to repeat the series of experiments of which we gave an account in the last chapter, but we lost no opportunity, during our long abode in the French possessions in India, and the different voyages we made in that vast country, of attentively observing any manifestations that bore any relation to that subject.

Leaving Chandernagor on the 3d of January, 1866, in a *dingui*, which is a sort of boat peculiar to that country, provided with a small cabin, I arrived at Benares, the Holy City, a fortnight afterward.

Two servants accompanied me, a *cansama*,[1] or valet-de-chambre, and a *metor*, whose duty it was to prepare my meals.

The crew consisted of a *cercar*, or head boatman, and six *macouas*, or rowers, belonging to the caste of fishermen.

Shortly before sunset one evening we were lying off the staircase of Gath near the celebrated pagoda of Siva. It is impossible to describe the spectacle that met my eyes.

"Few cities," says E. Roberts, "no matter how magnificent, are so grand and imposing in appearance as Benares."

When the watchful traveller ascends the Ganges his approach to the great city is first announced by the appearance of the minarets, whose towers, rising above the heavy masses of the surrounding palaces, are scattered in an apparently disorderly, though picturesque manner, along the crooked banks of the river, for about a couple of leagues.

It is impossible to resist the impression made by the magnificent panorama presented by such a multitude of temples, towers, long arcades supported by columns, elevated quays, and terraces whose balustrades stand out in strong relief, amid the luxuriant foliage of baobab, tamarind, and banana trees; and which, covered here and there with clusters of flowers of various shades, appearing among the heavily carved buildings, rise majestically above gardens, beautifully situated among spacious courts.

The absence of any regular plan, the different styles of architecture, the mingling of the austere and solemn with the light and fantastic, give an odd appearance to some parts of the scene, but its effect as a whole is magnificent, and most of the details possess a beauty of which it is impossible to give any conception.

---

[1] In Hindustanee the word *cansama* means the same as *dobachy* in Tamoul.

The gaths, which are a sort of monument composed of four columns united by a single cornice, and which are situated at the top of the gigantic stairs, whose bottom steps are bathed in the waters of the Ganges, are the only quays possessed by the old city, which was the ancient Kassy of the earliest rajahs. From the rising to the setting of the sun they are covered by coolies loading and unloading the small vessels that traverse the Ganges in every direction, bringing to market in upper Bengal all the merchandise of India and Asia.

As I ordered the cercar to moor the boat to the gath of Siva a circumstance struck me with astonishment. The Hindus and Mussulmans who, time out of mind, have been so deeply divided by their old enmity toward each other in the south of India, where they are an insignificant minority of the whole population, were performing their ablutions together promiscuously at the feet of the gaths of Benares.

Though the followers of the Prophet have always fought against idolatry with fire and sword, until the reign of Aurengzeb, they always respected the sacred city of their conquered foe, which seemed to inspire them with a mysterious terror.

The Brahmins claimed that Benares had been built by Siva, in order to serve as an asylum to the righteous, when the earth should be overrun by crime and sorrow; and that it would never experience any of those vicissitudes to which all earthly things are subject.

Aurengzeb, to humiliate their pride, destroyed one of their oldest and most venerable pagodas, and erected in its stead the splendid mosque that bears his name, whose slender spires, covered with leaves of gold, inform travellers that the city is at hand, long before they can see it. To-day, numerous Mussulman temples rise by the side of Hindu pagodas, and the Brahmins witness, without being able to prevent it, but with horror that they are powerless to conceal, the slaughter of cattle for sacrificial or culinary purposes in the holy city, which had been polluted by the killing of no animal since the Mogul invasion.

In spite of the vandalism which has destroyed some of the oldest and handsomest monuments in India, and although in other countries subject to their laws the Mussulmans have used every means and shrunk from nothing in order to convert the Hindus to the faith of the Prophet, the Mogul sovereigns always used the largest tolerance at Benares for the religious beliefs, manners, and usages of their conquered foe. It is for this reason, no doubt, that the two nations are on the best of terms in this part of Bengal. However, until I had seen it I would never have believed that the Mussulmans and Hindus would ever consent to perform their religious ablutions in the same place.

In the south of India, a Mussulman who should bathe in the sacred tank of a pagoda would be put to death on the spot.

When I arrived at Benares, I intended to remain there a couple of months. That was by no means too long a stay, in view of the inquiries I desired to make regarding the antiquities of the country, but it was too long to put up at a hotel or bungalow. I therefore determined to hire a house of my own and to go to housekeeping at once. To have a home of one's own in the East, and especially in the far East, is almost one of the first necessaries of life.

I was about sending my *cansama* upon a voyage of discovery, when the Peishwa, a Mahratta prince at Benares with whom I had become acquainted through the Rajah at Chandernagor, hearing of my arrival, sent to offer me apartments in the magnificent seven storied palace owned by him upon the banks of the Ganges, to the left of the celebrated mosque of Aurengzeb.

It is no uncommon thing for the princes and rajahs of

Hindustan, although they often reside at a great distance from Benares, to build houses in that city, to which they resort during the festivities incident to the celebration of their birthday, and to which they retire in the evening of life, when, weary of the world, they desire to end their days, according to the laws of Manu, in the observance of their religious duties and in the practice of austerity.

According to their religious belief, those who die in the Holy City are not obliged to go through any further transformations, but their souls immediately ascend to the abode of Brahma and are absorbed in the great soul.

Numerous pilgrims daily arrive from all parts of India, who come to perform, either on their own account, or on behalf of wealthy persons who employ and pay them for that purpose, devotional exercises, upon the banks of the sacred river, whose waters are nowhere else considered so propitious as at the feet of the Holy City.

Some bring the bones of Rajahs or other distinguished personages, whose families are able to afford the expense, which are collected after being burnt upon the funeral pyre *in little bags* which they are instructed to throw into the Ganges. The supreme hope of the Hindu is to die upon the banks of that river, or to transport his remains thither.

To this latter belief I was indebted, during my stay at Benares, for a meeting with the most extraordinary Fakir, perhaps, that I had ever encountered in India. He came from Trivanderam, near Cape Comorin, in the extreme south of Hindustan, and his mission was to take charge of the remains of a rich Malabar, belonging to the caste of *commoutys* (merchants). The Peishwa, whose family was originally from the South, and who was in the habit of extending hospitality to pilgrims from Travencor, Maissour, Tandjaor, and the old Mahratta country, in the buildings attached to his palace, had found lodgings for him in a small thatched cottage upon the very banks of the river in which he had to perform his ablutions, for the next three weeks, in honor of the dead. He had been there a fortnight already before I heard of his arrival. His name was Covindasamy.

After assuring myself of his consent, I had him brought to my apartment one day, at about noon, when the other occupants of the palace, on account of the extreme heat, were indulging in their noonday siesta.

The room in which I received him looked out upon the terrace, which in turn overlooked the Ganges, and was protected against the burning sun, by a movable tent made from woven fibres of vetivert. In the middle of the terrace there was a water-spout which fell in a fine shower into a marble basin and diffused a most delightful coolness.

I asked the Fakir if he wished to occupy any particular place, rather than another.

"As you please," he answered.

I asked him to go out upon the terrace, which was much lighter than the room, and where I would have a better opportunity to watch him.

"Will you allow me to put to you a single question?" said I, when he had assumed a squatting position upon the ground.

"I am listening to you."

"Do you know whether any power is developed in you, when you perform these phenomena? Did you ever feel any change take place in your brain or any of your muscles?"

"It is not a natural force that acts. I am but an instrument. I evoke the ancestral spirits, and it is they who manifest their power."

I have questioned a multitude of Fakirs in relation to this matter, and they have nearly all made the same answer. They look upon themselves only as intermediaries between this world and the invisible spirits. Observing that he entertained the same belief, I dropped the subject in order that Covindasamy might go on with his performances. The Fakir was already in position with both hands extended toward an immense bronze vase full of water. Within five minutes the vase commenced to rock to and fro upon its base, and approach the Fakir gently and with a regular motion. As the distance diminished, metallic sounds escaped from it, as if some one had struck it with a steel rod. At certain times the blows were so numerous and quick that they produced a sound similar to that made by a hail-storm upon a metal roof.

I asked Covindasamy if I could give directions, and he consented without hesitation.

The vase, which was still under the performer's influence, advanced, receded, or stood still, according to my request.

At one time, at my command, the blows changed into a continuous roll like that of a drum; at another, on the contrary, they succeeded each other with the slowness and regularity of the ticking of a clock.

I asked to have the blows struck only every ten seconds, and I compared them with the progress of the second hand upon the face of my watch.

Then loud, sharp strokes were heard, for a minute and two-thirds.

Upon the table of the drawing-room attached to my apartments, stood one of those music-boxes of which the Hindus are so fond, and which the Peishwa had no doubt procured from Calcutta. I had it brought out upon the terrace by my *cansama*, and I asked to have the blows struck upon the vase so as to accompany any air which the instrument might perform.

I then wound up the box in the usual way, and pressed the spring of the clock-work, without knowing what air it would play. A regular whirlwind of notes was the result, and the box played, in time designedly accelerated, no doubt, the tune of "Robin of the Wood."

I listened in the direction of the vase, and quick, sharp strokes accompanied the tune, with the regularity of the baton of an orchestra leader. The air had scarcely finished when I again pressed the spring, and the blows moderated their pace to keep time to the march from the *Prophête*, which they accompanied exactly.

All this was done without fuss, or parade, or mystery of any kind, upon a terrace of a few yards square. The vase thus put in motion, could hardly, when empty, have been moved by two men. It was hollowed out like a cup, and was so situated as to receive the falling jet of water from the fountain before spoken of. It was used for the morning ablutions, which, in India, are almost equal to a regular bath.

What was the force that moved this mass? that is the question.

I repeated these various experiments a second time, and they were renewed with like order and regularity.

The Fakir, who had neither changed his position, nor left his place, then stood up, and rested the tips of his fingers, for a short time, upon the edge of the vase. It soon began to rock to and fro in regular time, from left to right, gradually accelerating its speed; its base, which rose and fell alternately on either side, made no sound upon the stuccoed pavement.

But what surprised me most was to see that the water remained stationary in the vase, as if there were a strong pressure that prevented its regaining its equilibrium, which the motion of the vessel containing it had disturbed.

Three times during these oscillations the vase rose a distance of seven to eight inches completely from the ground, and, when it fell to the pavement again, it did so without any perceptible shock.

The performance had already lasted several hours, during which I had taken copious and careful notes, and had also taken the precaution to have each phenomenon re peated in a different manner, when the sun, which was sinking below the horizon, warned us that it was time for me to commence my usual excursion among the venerable monuments and ruins of ancient Kassy, which was the centre of the religious power of the Brahmins when, after their contest with the rajahs, they had lost their temporal power—as well as for the Fakir to prepare himself in the temple of Siva, by the usual prayers, for the ablutions and funeral ceremonies which he was obliged to perform every evening, upon the banks of the sacred river.

Upon taking his departure the Fakir promised to return every day, at the same hour, as long as he should remain at Benares.

The poor man was very glad to have met me. I had resided for many years in the south of India, and knew the beautiful and sonorous language of the country of Bravida,[1] which no one else understood at Benares. He had now some one to talk to about this wonderful land and its ancient ruins, its old pagodas and their incomparable vegetation, and its manuscripts, written with a pointed stick centuries before the sea had abandoned the salt deserts of Iran and Chaldea, or the mud deposits of the Nile had joined Lower Egypt to the plains of Memphis and Thebes.

---

[1] The Tamoul.

CHAPTER VI.

THE WATER-SPOUT—THE MAGIC STICK.

Covindasamy was punctual in the performance of his engagement.

Gazing at the extraordinary flood of light which the sun poured upon the surface of the Ganges as it rolled by, I stood absorbed in silent contemplation of the magnificent spectacle before me, when the Fakir, lifting one of the curtains which hung before the door leading into the verandah, walked in and sat upon the floor with his legs bent under him after the Hindu manner.

"Salam béré" (good day, sahib), said he, using his mother tongue.

"Salam tambi" (good day, friend), replied I, in the same idiom, "is the Bengal rice equal to the rice of Tandjaor?"

"The rice served to me in the Peishwa's palace at Benares is not equal to that which I gather about my hut at Trivanderam."

"What is the matter with it? is not the curry seed as pure upon the banks of the Ganges as upon the Malabar coast?"

"Listen! the cocoa-tree does not grow here and the water of the sacred river cannot take the place of the salt water. I am a man of the coast, as there is a tree of the coast, and we both of us die when we are separated from the ocean."

Just then a slight southern breeze like escaping steam swept in warm gusts over the drowsy city slumbering in the noon-day heat. The Fakir's eyes glistened.

"It comes from my old home," said he, "do you not feel it? it brings to my mind so many recollections."

He sat a long while, thinking, no doubt, of the wide, gloomy forests on the Malabar coast, where he had passed his childhood, and of the mysterious caves of the pagoda at Trivanderam, where the Brahmins had instructed him in the art of evocation.

Suddenly he arose and walked toward the bronze vase which he had used the day before for the purpose of exhibiting his power. He imposed his hands upon the surface of the water which filled it to the very edge, but he did not touch it, however, and stood motionless in that position. As yet I had no idea of the phenomena that he intended to perform.

I do not know that he experienced any unusual difficulty on that day, but an hour had elapsed before either the water or the vase exhibited any evidence whatever of action on his part.

I had begun to despair of obtaining any result on that occasion, when the water began to be gently agitated. It looked as though its surface were ruffled by a slight breeze. Placing my hands upon the edge of the vase I experienced a slight feeling of coolness, which apparently arose from the same cause. A rose-leaf, thrown into the water, soon was blown or drifted against the other edge.

Meanwhile the Fakir stood motionless. His mouth was closed, and, strange to say, though it effectually disposed of any idea of trickery on his part, the waves were formed on the opposite side from that of the performer and gently broke against the edge of the vase on his side.

Gradually the motion of the waves became more violent. They made their appearance in every direction, as though the water were in a state of intense ebullition under the influence of a great heat. It soon rose higher than the Fakir's hands, and several waves rose to a height of one or two feet from the surface.

I asked Covindasamy to take his hands away. Upon their removal the motion of the water gradually abated, without ceasing altogether, as in the case of boiling water from which the fire has been removed. On the other hand, whenever he placed his hands in their former position, the motion of the water was as great as ever.

The last portion of the séance was still more extraordinary.

The Hindu asked me to lend him a small stick. I handed him a wooden lead-pencil that had never been sharpened. He placed it in the water, and in a few minutes, by the imposition of his hands, he made it move in every direction, like a magnet in contact with an iron bar.

Placing his forefinger gently upon the middle of the pencil, so as not to affect its position upon the water, in a few minutes I saw the small piece of wood slowly descend beneath the surface, until it had reached the bottom of the vase.

Laying aside the question of skill or deception on the performer's part, without doing which it is impossible for me to make any positive statement either one way or the other, although under the circumstances it would have been extremely difficult for any attempt at imposture to have escaped my attention, it occurred to me that the Fakir, upon charging the small piece of wood with fluid, might perhaps have increased its weight, so as to make it heavier than water.

Though deeply sceptical with regard to spirits, I often wondered, whenever I saw an experiment of this kind, whether or not some natural force had not been brought into play, with which we were totally unacquainted.

I merely state the facts without further comment.

CHAPTER VII.

PHENOMENA OF ELEVATION AND KNOCKING.

The Fakir's third visit was short, as he was to pass the night in prayer upon the banks of the sacred river, upon the occasion of a religious festival, and he had been invited to a funeral sraddha, which was to take place on the following day.

He came merely to inform me that he would be obliged to attend them, and was preparing to return to the small hut that the Peishwa had given him the use of, when, at my request, he consented to perform a phenomenon of elevation, which I had already seen other performers successfully accomplish, without, however, taking any particular notice of how they did it.

Taking an ironwood cane which I had brought from Ceylon, he leaned heavily upon it, resting his right hand upon the handle, with his eyes fixed upon the ground. He then proceeded to utter the appropriate incantations, which he had forgotten to favor me with the day previous.

From the elaborate preparation he made in my presence, I formed the opinion that this was to be only another instance of what I had always regarded as an acrobatic trick.

My judgment refuses, in fact, to attach any other name to such phenomena as this:

Leaning upon the cane with one hand, the Fakir rose gradually about two feet from the ground. His legs were crossed beneath him, and he made no change in his position, which was very like that of those bronze statues of

Buddha that all tourists bring from the far East, without a suspicion that most of them come originally from English foundries.

For more than twenty minutes I tried to see how Covindasamy could thus fly in the face and eyes of all the known laws of gravity; it was entirely beyond my comprehension; the stick gave him no visible support, and there was no apparent contact between that and his body, except through his right hand.

When I dismissed him he informed me, upon leaving, that when the sacred elephants should strike the hour of midnight upon the copper gong in the pagoda of Siva, he would evoke the familiar spirits that protect the Franguys (or French), who would then manifest their presence in some manner in my bedroom.

The Hindus have a perfect understanding among themselves. In order to prevent any too obvious fraud, I sent my two servants to pass the night upon the dingui with the cercar and boatmen. The idea of the supernatural was naturally repugnant to my mind. My leanings were all the other way, but if the fact should occur as he predicted, I did not want to be too easily duped. For that reason I prepared to throw every obstacle in the Fakir's way.

The Peishwa's house was singularly constructed; all the windows overlooked the Ganges, and it contained seven large apartments, one above the other. All the rooms in each apartment opened upon covered galleries or terraces projecting over the quay. The mode of communication from one story to another was very curious. There was a single flight of steps which led from the bottom apartment to that immediately above. Upon crossing this second apartment, in the last room was a second flight of stairs which had no communication with the former, and which led to the story above, and so on up to the seventh story, which was reached by means of a movable stairway which could be raised by chains like a drawbridge.

It was this seventh story, which was furnished in a style partly Oriental and partly European, which commanded a most splendid view and where the air was the coolest, that the Peishwa had set apart for his foreign guests.

As soon as it was dark, I examined all the different rooms in the apartment, in the most careful manner, and made sure that nobody was concealed in them. I then raised the drawbridge, and thus cut off all communication from the outside.

At the hour named I thought I heard two blows distinctly struck against the wall of my room. I walked toward the spot from which the sound seemed to come, when my steps were suddenly arrested by a sharp blow, which appeared to proceed from the glass shade that protected the hanging lamp against gnats and night butterflies. A few more sounds were heard at unequal intervals in the cedar rafters of the ceiling, and that was all. I walked toward the end of the terrace. It was one of those silvery nights, unknown in our more foggy lands. The vast flood of the sacred river rolled silently along at the foot of the sleeping city, upon one of whose steps the outlines of a human form were dimly profiled. It was the Fakir of Trivanderam, praying for the repose of his dead.

CHAPTER VIII.

THE BAMBOO STOOL—AËRIAL FLOWERS—THE MYSTERIOUS PUNKAH.

I spent a part of the night in reflection upon this subject, but I was not able to solve the riddle. Since I had lived in India I had often seen similar phenomena performed in my presence by others and I was able to bring a multitude of other facts quite as wonderful to the support of what was said and done by the Fakir of Trivanderam, but they did not prove, in my opinion, the truth of the theory with regard to the evocation of the ancestral shades. What I beg to direct the reader's attention to, more particularly because it is strictly true, is the fact that the means employed to produce these phenomena are not known to any person in India except the performers themselves.

I was impatiently expecting the Fakir's arrival, for I had long intended to accompany my investigations into the ancient doctrine regarding the Pitris with an inquiry into the material phenomena inseparably connected, in the Hindu mind, with their religious convictions. The willingness, added to the skill, of Covindasamy gave me an opportunity that might not soon occur again of reviewing these singular facts, which seem to have occupied the minds of the sacerdotal classes in ancient times in all their leisure moments, and which had been repeated in my presence more than a hundred times before. I spent a portion of the day in visiting the temples and mosques of Benares, and I did not not return to the palace until sunset.

It was night, and I was waiting for the Fakir upon the terrace when he walked quietly in. People of that class have the privilege of entering the presence of the highest personages in Hindustan at any time, without previous announcement, and although they seldom make use of the privilege in the case of Europeans, I had, in the beginning of our acquaintance, allowed Covindasmy to do as he pleased. This, added to my knowledge of his native tongue, had made him very friendly.

"Well," said I, "as soon as I perceived his entrance, "the sounds were heard as you predicted; the Fakir is very skilful."

"The Fakir is nothing," he answered, with the utmost coolness. "He utters the proper mentrams and the spirits hear them. It was the ancestral shades of the Franguy who paid him a visit."

"Have you power over the spirits of foreigners?"

"No one has power over the spirits."

"I did not express myself properly. How does it happen that the souls of the Franguys should grant the requests of a Hindu? They do not belong to your caste."

"There are no castes in the superior world."

"Then it was my ancestors who appeared last night?"

"You have said it."

Such was his invariable answer.

Whenever I questioned him upon this subject I carefully watched the expression of his face, to see if I could detect in his looks a smile or any other sign of incredulity, but he seemed to be sincere, and his face was calm and impenetrable.

Without being asked to do so, he then went on with his performances.

Taking a small bamboo stool that stood near, he sat down upon it in the Mussulman style with his legs crossed beneath him, and his arms folded across his chest.

According to my instructions to my cansama, the ter

race had been lighted *à giorno*, and I had made such preparations that nothing that occurred could possibly escape my attention.

As in my accounts of previous performances, I omit all the elaborate preparations by which they were accompanied, and the impression made upon my own mind, and confine myself strictly to what is essential.

At the end of a few minutes, during which he appeared to concentrate his attention upon the bamboo stool upon which he was sitting, it began to move noiselessly along the floor, by short jerks which made it advance about three or four inches every time. I watched the Hindu attentively, but he was as still and motionless as a statue.

The terrace was about seven yards long and as many wide. It took about ten minutes to traverse the whole distance, and when the stool had arrived at the end it began to move backward until it returned to its starting-place. The performance was repeated three times, and always successfully, unless the conditions were changed. I ought to say, however, that the Fakir's legs, which were crossed beneath him, were distant from the ground the whole height of the stool.

During the whole day the heat had been overpowering. The night breeze which springs up so regularly in those latitudes to cool the heated lungs, and which blows from the Himalaya Mountains, had not yet risen. The metor was moving, as fast as he could, by the aid of a rope of cocoa fibre above our heads, an enormous punkah, hanging from iron rods in the middle of the terrace, which also supported horizontally the vetivert curtains and surrounding matting.

The punkah is a sort of movable fan of rectangular form, which is fastened at both ends to the ceiling of the room. Set in motion by a servant specially engaged for that purpose, it imparts a factitious, though very agreeable, coolness to the atmosphere. The Fakir made use of this instrument for the performance of the second phenomenon.

Taking the punkah rope from the metor's hands, he pressed it against his forehead with both hands, and sat down in a squatting position beneath the punkah, which soon began to move slowly over our heads, though Covindasamy had not made the slightest motion. It gradually increased its speed until it moved at a very rapid rate, as though it were driven by some invisible hand.

When the Fakir let go of the rope it continued to move, though at a gradually diminishing rate, and finally stopped altogether.

These two phenomena were repeated several times, and it was now quite late at night, but the Fakir was in a good humor, and before leaving he determined to give me another proof of his power.

Three vases of flowers, so heavy that none but a strong man could have lifted them (and then he could not have done so without an effort), stood at one end of the terrace. Selecting one, he imposed his hands upon it so as to touch the edge of the vase with the tips of his fingers. Without any apparent effort on his part it began to move to and fro upon its base as regularly as the pendulum of a clock. It soon seemed to me that the vase had left the floor, without changing its movement in the least degree, and it appeared to me to be floating in the air, going from right to left at the will of the Fakir.

I do not, it will be observed, speak of this phenomenon in positive terms, for I have always regarded it as caused by an illusion of the senses. To be candid, I must acknowledge that I have always been somewhat sceptical with regard to the phenomena performed by the Fakirs, but that especially, though I had often seen it performed under circumstances that seemed to render deception impossible, always appeared to me so strange that I was unable to resist the belief that some imposition, however elaborate or skilful, was being practised upon me.

CHAPTER IX.

THE STATIONARY TABLE—A SHOWER OF KNOCKS—THE LITTLE MILL—FLYING FEATHERS—THE HARMONIFLUTE.

Covindasamy had only three days more to stay at Benares. I determined to devote our last meeting to experiments in *magnetism and somnambulism*. When I informed him of my intention he seemed to be surprised by these novel expressions, though I translated them as well as I could into the Tamoul language.

When I had made him understand the meaning attached to those words in Europe, he smiled and answered, in his usual way, that such phenomena were also produced by the Pitris, in addition to those I had already witnessed. It was not possible to hold any discussion with him upon that point. Without regard to his religious opinions, or to the causes to which he attributed his power, I merely asked him if he was willing to take part in experiments of that character.

"The Franguy," he answered, "has spoken to the Fakir in his native language. The Fakir can refuse him nothing."

Seeing that his reply was so satisfactory in this respect, I was encouraged to make another request.

"Will you allow me to-day," said I, "to indicate the phenomena that I wish you to perform, instead of leaving them to you?"

Although it seems highly improbable, in view of the peculiar circumstances of their occurrence, that the Fakir should have made any preparations in advance for the performances which I have already described, or should have had any previous understanding with the servants, I was anxious, however, to ascertain whether Covindasamy would be able to produce any manifestations that he had no previous notice of.

"I will do as you please," said the Hindu, simply. This plan however, met the fate of many others. I spent so much time, and took so deep an interest in the Fakir's manifestations of spiritual force, that I had no opportunity to investigate the subject of his magnetic power.

I had often seen the performing Fakirs attach different objects to the ground, either, according to the explanation given me by an English major who had devoted much time and thought to questions of this class, by charging them with fluid in order to augment their specific gravity or in some other manner unknown to me. I determined to repeat the experiment. Taking a small stand of teak wood which I could lift without any effort with my thumb and forefinger, I placed it in the middle of the terrace, and asked the Fakir if he could not fix it there so that it could not be moved.

The Fakir, without the slightest hesitation, walked toward the small piece of furniture, and imposing both hands upon the top stood motionless in that position for nearly a quarter of an hour, at the end of which time he said to me, smiling:

The spirits have come and nobody can remove the table without their permission.

Feeling somewhat incredulous, I approached the table and took hold of it, as though I were going to lift it. It would not stir from the ground any more than if it had been sealed. I struggled harder, with the result that the fragile leaf there fastened came off in my hands.

I then took hold of the legs, which were united by a cross brace and which remained standing, but the result was the same. A thought then crossed my mind.

Suppose, thought I, that these phenomena are produced by the Fakir's charging objects with some kind of fluid, and that a natural force is thus developed the laws of which we are as yet ignorant of, the supply of fluid with which they are charged must gradually lose its efficacy unless renewed by the operator, and in that case I shall soon be able to remove what is left of the table without any difficulty.

I asked the Fakir to go to the other end of the terrace, which he did with the utmost good humor imaginable. At the end of a few minutes I was able to handle the stand without any trouble whatever. It was evident, therefore, that there was a force of some kind or other; there was no other alternative unless I was willing to admit that I had been egregiously imposed upon, which would have been impossible, under the circumstances.

I should have had to devote some months to this experiment alone, if I had desired to test it scientifically. I had not sufficient time at my disposal to do so, and I merely describe it now, like all the rest, without expressing an opinion either one way or the other, as to means employed or the cause thereof.

"The Pitris have departed," said the Hindu, in explanation, "because their means of terrestrial communication was broken. Listen! they are coming back again."

As he uttered these words, he imposed his hands above one of those immense copper platters inlaid with silver such as are used by wealthy natives for dice playing, and almost immediately there ensued such a rapid and violent succession of blows or knocks that it might have been taken for a hail-shower upon a metal roof, and I thought I saw (the reader will observe that I do not express myself positively in this respect) a succession of phosphorescent lights (plain enough to be visible in broad daylight) pass to and fro across the platter in every direction.

This phenomenon ceased or was repeated at the Fakir's pleasure.

I have already remarked that the apartments I occupied at the Peishwa's were furnished partly in the European and partly in the Oriental style. There was a multitude of fancy articles upon the étagères, such as windmills setting blacksmiths in motion, tin soldiers, and wooden houses from Nuremberg with those everlasting little green fir trees, from which many children obtain their earliest ideas of nature. The furniture was all cluttered up with objects of this nature; the most childish articles were mingled pell-mell with the most artistic, according to the fancies of the native servants. We need not laugh, however; a native of those countries could not look at three-quarters of the Chinese, Hindu, or Oceanic objects with which we proudly and ostentatiously decorate our dwellings, and keep a sober face. I bethought myself of a small mill which might be moved by a breath, which set several personages in motion. I pointed it out to Covindasamy and asked him if he could make it go without touching it.

In consequence of the imposition of his hands alone he set the mill in motion with great rapidity, at a rate which increased or diminished according to the distance at which the Fakir stood.

This was a very simple fact, but yet it made a great impression upon my mind, by reason of the improbability of any previous notice or preparation.

The following is another of the same character, but much more surprising.

Among the objects that composed the Peishwa's museum was a harmoniflute. By the aid of a small cord tied around the wooden square forming a portion of the bellows (a part of the instrument which, as everybody knows, is on the side opposite to that of the keys) I hung it from one of the iron bars of the terrace, in such a way that it swung in the air at about two feet from the ground, and I asked the Fakir if he could make it play without touching it.

Complying unhesitatingly with my request, he seized the cord by which the harmoniflute was suspended, between the thumb and forefinger of each hand and stood perfectly motionless and still. The harmoniflute soon began to be gently stirred, the bellows underwent an alternate movement of contraction and inflation, as though proceeding from some invisible hand, and the instrument emitted sounds which were perfectly plain and distinct, though of unusual length and not very harmonious it is true.

"Cannot you get a tune?" said I to Covindasamy.

"I will evoke the spirit of one of the old pagoda musicians," he answered with the greatest gravity.

I waited patiently.

The instrument had been silent a long while, not having made a sound since my request. It now began to move anew and first played a series of notes or chords like a prelude; it then bravely attacked one of the most popular airs on the Malabar coast.

Taïtou moncouty conda
Arouné cany pomelé, etc.

("Bring jewels for the young maiden of Arouné, etc.)

As long as the piece lasted the Fakir stood perfectly still. He merely had hold, as I have already described, of the cord by which he was in communieation with the harmoniflute.

Wishing to apply every test in my power, I kneeled down in order to observe the various movements of the instrument, and I saw, so that I am positively sure of what I say, unless I was misled by an illusion of the senses, the upward and downward motion of the keys, according to the requirements of the tune.

As before, I merely state the fact, and leave the reader to draw his own conclusions.

Suppose that there was no *illusion of the senses* and no *imposture* used in the production of these manifestations —shall we, in that case, investigate their laws?

No! say the French scientists, who occupy an official station, *à priori* such folly is not worthy of an investigation.

Yes! answer the scientists of England, who are not less dignified, we have ascertained material facts, which are free from the suspicion of *illusion or imposture.* We are bound in honor to ascertain their laws and proclaim the truth.

Such is the state of the question.

On the one hand, negation under any circumstances; on the other, further investigation.

Our French *savants—to call them by the name which they use among themselves*—have never lost sight, as we see, of the traditions which have led to the rejection of all the great inventions by which the present century has been distinguished.

I have not taken a very active part in the discussion and that for an obvious reason. Anybody might say to me, if I attempted to formulate a law governing the facts which have come under my own observation:

Have you experimented scientifically regarding all the extraordinary facts described as having been performed by the Fakirs?

As I have had manufactured under my own supervision neither the weights nor scales nor vases nor tables nor any of the instruments used by the Fakirs, to this question I am bound to answer—*scientifically* no!

But, on the other hand, when I see the Fakirs often using articles belonging to myself and most frequently things which, in all probability, they had never seen or touched before, I say with Messrs Crookes, Huggins, Cox, and others—here are the facts for your investigation, science should know the grounds upon which they rest before rejecting or accepting them.

At sunset Covindasamy was to perform his devotions upon the banks of the sacred river. It was near that hour now, and upon taking leave of me with the usual salaams he informed me that he could not come the next day.

As I expressed my regret, he answered me:

"To-morrow will be the twenty-first day since my arrival at Benares, and the mortuary ceremonies will then be concluded." The Fakir was to remain at prayer from one sunrise to another—a period of twenty-four hours. When his task was accomplished, and previous to his departure for Trivanderam, he promised to give me an entire day and night, for, said he, "you have been very kind, and with you I could speak the language that my old ama (mother) used to speak when she rocked me to sleep in a banana leaf. My mouth has long been closed." He often recurred to this subject, and always seemed much moved when he spoke of it.

I have never known a Hindu to speak of his mother without emotion.

As he was about stepping across the threshold of the terrace door he noticed a vase containing various feathers, taken from the most wonderful birds in India. He took up a handful, which he threw above his head high in the air. The feathers of course descended again soon, but the Fakir made passes beneath them as they fell, and whenever one came near him, it turned around quickly and ascended again with a spiral movement, until stopped by the vetivert carpet, which answered the purpose of a movable roof. They all went in the same direction, but after a moment, in obedience to the laws of gravity, they dropped again, but before they had travelled half the distance to the ground they resumed their ascending movement and were stopped as before by the matting, where they remained.

A final tremor was followed by a slight manifestation of downward tendency, but the feathers soon remained stationary. If any one had seen them standing out in sharp relief against the golden background of the straw matting, in brilliant and decided colors of every possible shade, he would have said that they were placed there by the pencil of some accomplished artist.

As soon as the Fakir had disappeared they fell flat to the ground. I left them a long while as they lay strewn upon the floor, as a proof, of which I felt the need, that I had not been misled by some mental hallucination.

Night had no sooner come with its refreshing coolness, than I embarked upon the dingui which lay at the quay, and ordered the cercar to let the boat drift down the river with the current. Influenced, in spite of myself, by the incomprehensible phenomena which I had just witnessed, I felt as though I wanted to change my surroundings, instead of groping my way dreamily among the metaphysical speculations of the past. I also felt the need of the pleasanter sensations always accompanying a night upon the Ganges, soothed by the song of the Hindu boatmen and the distant cry of savage beasts.

CHAPTER X.

SAND DRAWING—THE METOR AND THE BUCKET OF WATER—LOSS OF VOICE—MIND READING—READING IN A CLOSED BOOK—AËRIAL MELODY—THE FLYING PALM-LEAF—ELEVATION OF THE FAKIR.

Covindasamy had promised me that before he left to return to Trivanderam he would employ all the power at his command, or, to use an expression for which he alone is responsible, *he would appeal to all the Pitris who assisted him*, and would show me something wonderful that I would never forget.

On the day in question we were to have two sittings, one in the broad light of day, like those which I have previously described, and one at night, but I was to be free to illuminate the place in which the experiments were to be held as much as I pleased.

The gath of Siva was hardly gilded by the first rays of the rising sun when the Hindu, whose mission was now at an end, sent in his name by my cansama. He was afraid that he would find me asleep.

"Saranai-aya" (greeting, sahib), said he, upon entering. To-morrow is the day of the Fakir's return to the land of his ancestors.

"My best wishes will accompany you," answered I. "I hope that you will find that your abode has been respected by the evil spirits during your absence."

As usual, the Fakir made no attempt to continue the conversation. He immediately sat down upon the ground, after the ordinary salutation, and lost no time in beginning his performances.

He had brought with him a small bag of the finest sand, which he proceeded to empty upon the floor and level with his hand, in such a way as to form a surface of about half a square yard.

When he had done this, he asked me to sit at a table opposite him, with a sheet of paper and a pencil.

Having asked for a small piece of wood, I threw him the handle of a penholder, which he gently placed upon the bed of sand.

"Listen!" said he. "I am about to evoke the Pitris. When you see the article which you have just given me stand upright, one end only being in contact with the ground, you are at liberty to trace upon the paper any figures you please, and you will see an exact copy of them in the sand."

He then extended both hands before him horizontally, and proceeded to repeat the sacred formulas of evocation.

In a few minutes the wooden rod gradually rose as he had said, and at the same moment I proceeded to move my pencil over the sheet of paper before me, tracing the strangest figures in the world entirely at random. The piece of wood at once imitated every motion, and I saw the whimsical figures that I had been tracing appear successively in the sand.

When I stopped, the improvised pencil stopped—when I went on, it followed me.

The Fakir had not changed his position, and there was no apparent contact between him and the piece of wood.

Wishing to know whether he could see, from his position, the movements of the pencil, as I drew it over the sheet of paper, which however would not have explained how he could transfer the figures without being in contact with the sand upon which they appeared, I left the table, and placing myself in an identically similar position to that of Covindasamy, I was able to satisfy myself that it was totally impossible for him to ascertain what I was doing.

I then compared the figures with each other, and I found that they were exactly alike.

Having levelled the sand again, the Fakir said to me:

"Think of a word in the language of the gods"—the Sanscrit.

"Why that language particularly?" I answered.

"Because the Pitris use that immortal medium of speech more easily than any other. The impure are not allowed to use it."

I was not in the habit of disputing his religious convictions, and therefore said nothing.

The Hindu then extended his hands as before. The magic pencil began to move, and, gradually rising, wrote unhesitatingly the following word:

Pouroucha!
(The celestial generator).

That was actually the word that I had thought of.

"Think of a whole phrase," continued the Fakir.

"I have done so," I answered.

The pencil then wrote upon the sand the following words:

Adicêtê Veikountam Haris!
(Vischnou sleeps upon Mount Eikonta).

"Can the spirit by whom you are inspired give me the 243d sloca of the fourth book of Manu?" inquired I of Covindasamy.

I had hardly expressed the wish, when the pencil proceeded to gratify it, and wrote the following words one after the other, letter by letter, before my eyes:

Darmaprâdânam pouroucham tapasa' hatakilvisam paralôkam nayaty âçou bâsouantam Kaçarîrinam.

The following is a translation of this remarkable stanza, which was correctly given as indicated:

* * *

"The man, the end of all whose actions is virtue, and all whose sins are wiped out by acts of piety and sacrifices, reaches the celestial mansions, radiant with light and clothed with a spiritual form."

Finally, as a last experiment, placing my hands upon a closed book containing extracts from hymns in the Rig-Veda, I asked for the first word of the fifth line of the twenty-first page. I received the following answer:

Dêvadatta.

(Given by a god.)

Upon comparison I found it to be correct.

"Will you now put a mental question?" said the Fakir.

I acquiesced by a simple movement of the head, and the following word was written upon the sand:

Vasundarâ.

(The Earth.)

I had asked, "Who is our common mother?"

I have no explanation or statement to make with regard to these facts.

Whether it is purely a matter of skill or whether the performers are really inspired—that is a question which I do not undertake to decide. I only describe what I have seen and assert that the circumstances under which the facts occurred are accurately related. *Materially speaking*, I do not think it possible that any fraud could have been committed.

The first part of this sitting was somewhat long. I asked the Fakir to discontinue his performances for a few minutes, during which I walked to the end of the terrace, whither he followed me.

It might have been ten o'clock in the forenoon.

The waters of the Ganges shone like a mirror in the bright light of a hot day. Upon our left lay a large garden, in the midst of which there stood a well, from which a metor was unconcernedly drawing water, which he poured into a bamboo pipe, which in its turn supplied a bathing-room.

Covindasamy imposed his hands in the direction of the well, and the result was that, though the poor metor pulled upon the rope with all his might, it would no longer slip through the pulley.

When a Hindu meets with any impediment in his work, he at once attributes any obstacle that he cannot overcome to evil spirits, and immediately proceeds to chant all the magical incantations with which he is acquainted, for the knowledge of which he has often paid a high price.

The poor metor, of course, could not let slip so favorable an opportunity to use the knowledge he had obtained; but he had hardly chanted a few words in that sharp nasal tone which is so lacerating to the European ear, but which is inflicted upon it everywhere in the East, and particularly in the far East, in the name of music, when his voice died away in his throat and he found it impossible, though he made the strangest contortions, to articulate a single word.

After looking at this curious sight for a few moments, the Fakir dropped his hands and the metor recovered the use of his speech, while the rope performed its office as before.

Upon returning to the scene of our late experiments, I found the heat to be overpowering and so remarked to the Fakir, who did not seem to hear me, absorbed as he was, apparently, in his own reflections. I had forgotten the remark that I had incidentally let drop, when one of those palm-leaf fans that Hindu servants use to cool the air in rooms where there is no punkah, flew up from the table, where it had been lying, and gently fanned my face.

I observed that, although it moved very slowly, the air was unusually cool and refreshing. At the same time, the atmosphere seemed to be filled with the melodious sounds of a human voice, which had nothing Hindu about it, which I thought I heard, like those faint songs that huntsmen on the mountains often hear rising from the valleys at twilight.

The palm leaf finally returned to the table and the sounds ceased. I wondered whether there had not been some illusion of my senses. As the Fakir was about to leave me, to go to his breakfast and obtain a few hours rest, of which he stood in urgent need, having had no food nor sleep for the last twenty-four hours, he stopped in the embrasure of the door leading from the terrace to the outside stairs, and, crossing his arms upon his chest, lifted himself up gradually, without any apparent support or assistance, to the height of about ten to twelve inches.

I was able to determine the distance exactly by means of a point of comparison which I had fixed upon during the continuance of the phenomenon. Behind the Fakir's back there was a silken hanging, which was used as a portière, striped in gold and white bands of equal width. I noticed that the Fakir's feet were on a level with the sixth band. At the commencement of his ascension I had seized my chronometer; the entire time from the moment when the Fakir commenced to rise until he touched the ground again, was more than eight minutes. He remained perfectly still, at the highest point of elevation for nearly five minutes.

As Covindasamy was making his parting salaam, I asked

if he could repeat the last phenomenon whenever he pleased.

"The Fakir," answered he, emphatically, "can lift himself up as high as the clouds."

"What is the source of his power?" I do not know why I asked him the question, as he had already told me, more than twenty times, that he did not regard himself as anything more than an instrument in the hands of the Pitris.

He answered me with the following lines:

Swâdyâyê nityayoukta' syât
Ambarâd avatarati dêva'.

"He should be in constant communication with heaven, and a superior spirit should descend therefrom."

CHAPTER XI.

SPONTANEOUS VEGETATION.

Huc, the missionary, in his account of his travels in Thibet, gives a description of a phenomenon similar to that which I am about to relate, and which I can only look upon as a cunning trick.

I should not have mentioned it, perhaps, in the present work, but it forms an essential part, so to speak, of the stock in trade of those believers in the Pitris, who deal more particularly in external manifestations, and, as a faithful historian, I am loath to omit any of their curious practices.

Among the extraordinary claims advanced by the Fakirs, is one that they can directly influence the growth of plants, and that they can so hasten it as to accomplish in a few hours what usually takes several months or even years.

I had already seen this phenomenon performed by itinerant magicians a number of times, but, as I had always regarded it merely as a successful fraud, I had omitted to record the circumstances under which it occurred.

Absurd as it seemed, as Covindasamy, who was really a man of remarkable power, proposed to repeat the various phenomena which I had already seen performed by others at different times, I determined to watch him so that he could do nothing which should escape my notice.

He had promised to give me two hours more of his time—from three to five—previous to the night sitting. I determined to employ them as proposed.

The Fakir suspected nothing, and I thought he would be highly surprised when, upon his arrival, I told him what I intended to.

"I am entirely at your service," said he, in his usual simple way.

I was somewhat disconcerted by his assurance, but I continued:

"Will you allow me to choose the earth, the vessel, and the seed, which you are to make grow before my eyes?"

"The vessel and the seed, yes; but the earth must be taken from a nest of carias."

These little white ants, who build, for shelter, small hills, often reaching a height of nine or a dozen yards, are very common in India, and there was no difficulty, whatever, in procuring a little of the earth which they prepare very skilfully for their purpose.

I told my cansama to have a flower-pot of the usual size filled with the earth required, and to bring me, at the same time, some seeds of different sorts.

The Fakir asked him to break the earth between a couple of stones, as it was only to be obtained in pieces, almost as hard as old building material.

It was well he did so, as that was an operation that we never could have performed in our rooms, without a great deal of trouble.

In less than a quarter of an hour my servant had returned with the articles required. I took them from his hands and dismissed him, not wishing to leave him in communication with Covindasamy.

To the latter I handed the flower-pot filled with a whitish earth, which must have been entirely saturated with that milky fluid, which the caria secrete and deposit upon every particle of earth, however small, which they use for building purposes.

When the Fakir deemed that it was in proper condition, he asked me to give him the seed that I had selected, as well as about a foot and a half of some white cloth. I chose at random a papaw seed from among those which my cansama had brought, and before handing it to him, I asked him if he would allow me to mark it. Being answered in the affirmative, I made a slight cut in its outer skin. It was very much like the kernel of a gourd, except in color, which was a deep brown. I gave it to him, with a few yards of mosquito cloth.

"I shall soon sleep the sleep of the spirits," said Covindasamy; "you must promise me that you will neither touch me personally nor the flower-pot."

I made the promise required.

He then planted the seed in the earth, which was now in a state of liquid mud, thrusting his seven-knotted stick—which, being a sign of his initiation, he never laid aside—into one corner of the vessel, and using it as a prop to hold up the piece of muslin which I had just given him. After hiding from sight in this manner the object upon which he was to operate, he sat down upon the floor, stretched both hands horizontally above him, and gradually fell into a deep cataleptic sleep.

I had promised that I would not touch him, and at first I could not tell whether his sleep was real or simulated; but when I saw, at the end of half an hour, that he had not stirred, I was forced to believe the evidence of my own senses. No man, however strong he might be, was able, except in that condition, to hold both his arms stretched horizontally before him for the space of even ten minutes.

An hour passed by, and no motion of the muscles indicated that he was alive. With his body almost entirely naked, his skin polished and glistening in the heat, and open and staring eyes, the Fakir looked like a bronze statue in a position of mystical evocation.

At first, I took my place opposite him, so that I could see everything that was going on, but he looked at me in a manner that soon became unendurable. His eyes seemed to be half dead, but they were filled at the same time with magnetic influences. At one time, everything seemed to be in a whirl, and the Fakir himself appeared to take part in the dance that was going on around me. In order to break loose from the effects of this hallucination of the senses, caused, no doubt, by looking at one object too attentively, I left the seat that I had been occupying, without, however, losing sight of Covindasamy, who was as motionless as a corpse. I took a seat at the end of the terrace, alternately directing my attention to the course of the Ganges and to the Fakir, that I might not be exposed to too direct and steady an influence from him.

I had been waiting for a couple of hours, and the sun was fast sinking below the horizon, when a low sigh startled me. The Fakir had recovered possession of his senses.

He made signs to me to approach. Removing the muslin that hid the flower-pot, he then pointed out to me a young stalk of papaw, fresh and green, and nearly eight inches high.

Anticipating my thoughts, he thrust his fingers into the ground, which, meanwhile, had parted with nearly all of its moisture, and carefully taking up the young plant, he showed me, upon one of the two cuticles still adhering to the roots, the cut that I had made two hours previously.

Was it the same seed and the same cut? I have only one answer to make. I noticed no substitution. The Fakir had not left the terrace; I had not lost sight of him. When he came, he did not know what I was going to ask. It was impossible for him to conceal a plant in his clothes, as he was almost entirely naked, and, at any rate, he could not have told, in advance, that I would select a papaw seed, among thirty different kinds that my cansama had brought.

As may be imagined, I can state nothing more positively

regarding a fact of this nature. There are cases where reason refuses its assent, even in view of phenomena that can only be accounted for upon the supposition of delusion, though there is no evidence to that effect.

After enjoying my surprise for a few moments, the Fakir said to me, with an ill-concealed movement of pride:

"If I had continued my evocations longer, the papaw tree would have borne flowers in eight days, and fruit in fifteen.

Bearing in mind the accounts of Huc, the missionary, as well as various other phenomena of the same character which I had myself witnessed in the Carnatic, I said in reply that there were other performers who accomplished the same results in two hours.

"You are mistaken," said the Hindu; "in the manifestations you speak of, there is an *apport*, as it is called, of fruit trees by the spirits. What I have just shown you is really *spontaneous vegetation;* but the pure fluid, under the direction of the Pitris, never was able to produce the three phases of germination, flowering, and fruitage in a single day."

It was near the hour of ablutions; in other words, it was near sunset. The Fakir hastened to leave, engaging to meet me, for the last time, at ten o'clock that evening, when the remainder of the night was to be devoted to phenomena of apparition.

There is one fact, however, which I ought not to omit, and which may be of service in arriving at a satisfactory explanation, and that is a fact with which those who live in India are perfectly familiar.

There are a multitude of kitchen plants (I have seen the experiment tried myself a score of times) which, when put at dawn into moist soil, and exposed to the favorable influence of a sun which does wonders, appear above ground between noon and one o'clock, and at six o'clock, or the close of day, are already nearly half an inch high.

On the other hand, I am bound also to say, in justice to the Fakir, at least fifteen days are necessary to the germination of a papaw seed.

We have dwelt long enough, however, on a fact which many will reject as a delusion, and which cannot be explained by any process of pure reasoning, excluding the hypothesis of fraud.

APPARITIONS.

CHAPTER I.

MYSTERIOUS HANDS—THE PRODUCTION OF FLOWERS, CROWNS, ETC.—LETTERS OF FIRE—THE SPECTRE OF A PRIEST OF BRAHMA—THE PHANTOM MUSICIAN.

Looking over my notes of travel, which were jotted down the next day, I see that they were written under the influence of the great excitement caused by the strange scenes that I had witnessed the day previous. I have simply undertaken to narrate facts as they occurred. If I should transcribe them as written, in the present work, I should be untrue to the character I have assumed.

If the reader is at all curious as to these singular manners and practices, he will find them described elsewhere [1] in all their details. As in the case of previous phenomena, my office is simply to report the facts that occurred during that surprising evening.

At the appointed hour Covindasamy quietly entered my room.

"Is not the Fakir fatigued by three weeks of watching and prayer?" said I, greeting him in the most friendly manner.

"The Fakir's body is never fatigued. It is a slave, whose only duty is obedience," answered the Hindu, sententiously.

Before entering my apartments, he had divested himself

[1] Travels among the performing Fakirs, 1 vol. in press, Dentu, Paris.

of the small piece of cloth, called the *langouty*, about four inches wide, which usually composed his only garment, and had deposited it upon one of the steps. He was entirely naked when he came in, and his seven-knotted stick was fastened to a lock of his long hair.

"Nothing impure" said he, "should come in contact with the body of the *evocator*, if he wishes to reserve his power of communication with the spirits unimpaired.

Whenever I met a Fakir of this character I wondered whether those whom the Greeks saw upon the banks of the Indus and whom they called γυμνοσοφισται, or naked monks, did not belong to the same class.

My bedroom was on a level with the terrace. I set apart both rooms for our experiments, and carefully shut and fastened all the outside doors by means of which they were accessible.

The terrace was securely closed by its movable ceiling and curtains of vetivert matting. There was no opening from the outside, and nobody could gain admission except through my bedroom.

In the centre of each room there was a cocoa oil-lamp, protected by a glass shade of the clearest crystal, which hung from a bronze chain and diffused a soft light, sufficiently intense, however, to enable any one to read the smallest type in the remotest corner of the room.

All Hindu houses contain small copper furnaces which are kept constantly supplied with burning coals, on which are burned from time to time a few pinches of a perfumed powder, consisting of sandal wood, iris root, incense and myrrh.

The Fakir placed one of these in the centre of the terrace, and deposited by its side a copper platter filled with the fragrant powder; having done so, he took his seat upon the floor in his usual posture, with his arms folded across his chest, and commenced a long incantation in an unknown tongue.

When he was through with the recitation of his mentrams, he remained in the same position without making a movement, his left hand resting upon his heart, and his right hand leaning upon his seven-knotted stick.

I thought that he was going to drop into a cataleptic sleep as he had done the day before, but such was not the case. From time to time, he pressed his hand against his forehead, and seemed to make passes as though to relieve his brain.

Involuntarily, I experienced a sudden shock. A slightly phosphorescent cloud seemed to have formed in the middle of my chamber, from which semblances of hands appeared to go and come with great rapidity. In a few minutes, several hands seemed to have lost their vaporous appearance and to resemble human hands; so much so, indeed, that they might have been readily mistaken for the latter. Singular to relate, while some became, as it were, more material, others became more luminous. Some became opaque, and cast a shadow in the light, while others became so transparent that an object behind them could be distinctly seen.

I counted as many as sixteen.

Asking the Fakir if I could touch them, I had hardly expressed a wish to that effect, when one of them, breaking away from the rest, flew toward me and pressed my outstretched hand. It was small, supple and moist, like the hand of a young woman.

"The spirit is present, though one of its hands is alone visible," said Covindasamy. "You can speak to it, if you wish."

I smilingly asked whether the spirit to whom that charming hand belonged would give me something in the nature of a keepsake.

Thereupon, in answer to my request, I felt the hand fade away in my own. I looked; it was flying toward a bouquet of flowers, from which it plucked a rosebud, which it threw at my feet and vanished.

For nearly two hours a scene ensued which was calculated to set my head in a whirl. At one time, a hand brushed against my face or fanned it with a fan. At another, it would scatter a shower of flowers all over the room, or would trace in the air, in characters of fire, words which vanished as soon as the last letter was written.

Some of these words were so striking that I wrote them down hastily with a pencil.

Divyavapour gatwâ.

Meaning in Sanscrit—"I have clothed myself with a fluidic (fluidique) body."

Immediately afterward, the hand wrote:

Atmânam crêyasa yoxyatas
Dehasya 'syá vimôcanant.

"You will attain happiness when you lay aside this perishable body."

Meanwhile, flashes of genuine lightning seemed to dart across both rooms.

Gradually, however, all the hands disappeared. The cloud from which they came seemed to vanish by degrees as the hands became more material.

In the place where the last hand had disappeared, we found a garland of those yellow flowers with penetrating fragrance which the Hindus use in all their ceremonies.

I offer no explanation—I merely relate what occurred—leaving the reader at perfect liberty to draw any conclusion that he may see fit.

I can state positively, however, that the doors of both rooms were closed, that I had the keys in my pocket, and that the Fakir had not changed his position.

To these phenomena succeeded two others, that were, perhaps, more surprising still.

Shortly after the hands had disappeared, and while the Fakir was still going on with his evocations, a cloud similar to the first, but more opaque and of a brighter color, hovered near the little furnace, which, at the Hindu's request, I had kept constantly fed with burning coals. By degrees it seemed to assume a human form, and I distinguished the spectre—for I cannot call it otherwise—of an old Brahminical priest kneeling by the side of the little furnace.

On his forehead he wore the signs of his consecration to Vischnou, while his body was girdled with the triple cord, which signified that he had been initiated into the priestly caste. He clasped his hands above his head as in the performance of sacrifices, and his lips moved as if they were reciting prayers. At a certain moment, he took a pinch of the perfumed powder and threw it upon the furnace; there must have been an unusual quantity, for the fire emitted a thick smoke which filled both rooms.

When the smoke dispersed, I noticed the spectre less than a couple of yards distant; it held out to me its fleshless hands. I took them in my own, as I returned his greeting, and was surprised to find them, though hard and bony, warm and lifelike.

"Are you really," said I, in a distinct voice, "a former inhabitant of the earth?"

I had hardly finished the question, when the word

Am
(meaning Yes),

appeared and disappeared in letters of fire upon the bosom of the old Brahmin. The effect was similar to that which would have been produced if the word had been written in the dark with a bit of phosphorus.

"Will you not leave me something as a token of your presence?"

The spirit broke the triple cord, consisting of three

strands of cotton, which was tied about his loins, gave it to me and then faded away before my eyes.

I supposed that the seance was over, and I was going to raise the movable curtains that shaded the terrace, to admit a little fresh air inside, where the heat was really suffocating, when I noticed that the Fakir seemed to have no such idea. All at once, I heard a strange tune performed upon an instrument, which seemed to be the harmoniflute that we had used a couple of days before. That, however, appeared impossible, inasmuch as the Peishwa had sent for it the day before, and it was consequently no longer in my rooms.

It sounded at a distance, at first, but soon it came so near that it appeared to come from the next room, and I seemed before long to hear it in my bedroom. I noticed the phantom of a musician from the pagodas, gliding along the wall. He had a harmoniflute in his hands, from which he drew plaintive and monotonous notes exactly like the religious music of the Hindus.

When he had made the circuit of my room and of the terrace, he disappeared, and I found the instrument that he had used at the very place where he had vanished.

It was actually the rajah's harmoniflute. I examined all the doors, but I found them all securely locked and I had the keys in my pocket.

Covindasamy then arose. All his limbs were covered with perspiration, and he seemed to be thoroughly exhausted, though, in a few hours, he was to set out on his return journey.

"Thanks, Malabar," said I, calling him by a name that he liked, because it reminded him of his native land. May he who possesses the *three mysterious powers*[1] protect you as you journey toward the fair land of the South, and may you find that joy and happiness have ruled in your cottage during your absence."

[1] The Brahminic trinity.

It is usual in India for people who are about to part to address each other in effusive and flowery terms, and I should have hurt the poor Fakir's feelings if I had spoken otherwise or had used plainer language, which he would have taken as a sign of indifference. He answered me in the same manner, but in even more exaggerated style, and, after accepting the presents that I offered him, without even looking at them or even deigning to thank me, he sorrowfully made his parting salaam and noiselessly disappeared behind the curtains that hung before the outside door to my rooms.

As soon as he had gone, I called my cansama, and ordered him to remove all the tattis and matting from the terrace, so as to admit the cool morning air.

In the pale light of approaching day, I noticed a black speck upon the silvery waves of the Ganges, as they rolled below, which seemed to move toward the opposite shore. I turned my night glass in that direction. It was the Fakir, who, as he had said, had awakened the ferryman and was crossing the Ganges on his homeward way to Trivanderam. A faint red streak in the distant sky indicated that the horizon would soon be illuminated by the beams of the rising sun.

He would soon see the ocean with its blue waves, his beloved cocoa-nut trees, and the cottage that he was constantly talking about.

I threw myself upon a hammock for a few hours' rest. When I awoke and remembered the strange scenes that had passed before my eyes, it seemed as though I had been the plaything of a dream. Yet there was the harmoni-flute, and I could not find out who, if anybody, had brought it. The floor of the terrace was still strewn with flowers, the crown of flowers was upon a divan, and the words that I had written had not vanished from the memorandum book in which I had jotted them down.

CHAPTER II.

THE PHANTOM OF KARLI.

About four years after this, I was travelling in the province of Aurungabad, on a visit to the subterranean temple of Karli, having come through Madras, Bellary, and Bedjapour.

These celebrated crypts, which are excavated from the living rock, are all situated within the area bounded by the Mahratta Hills, where are also found all the other monuments of this character that India possesses, as, for instance, Ellora, Elephanta, Rosah, etc.

According to E. Roberts, these hills, which all terminate in wide plateaux, were protected, at one time, by fortresses, which made this place a formidable line of defence against the Arabs and Mussulmans, which proved effectual for more than five centuries.

The ruins of citadels are still standing upon the steep road leading to Karli.

The entrance to the caves is situated about three hundred feet above the bottom of the hill, and the only access is by a rough and narrow path, which is more like the bed of a torrent than a practicable road.

The path leads to a terrace or platform, partly artificial, and cut in the rock, or built of fragments of rock taken from the inside.

It is about a hundred feet wide, and forms a square worthy of the magnificence of the interior of the temple.

At the left of the portico stands a massive column, supporting, upon its capital, three lions so disfigured by the hand of time that they can with difficulty be recognized at all. This column is covered with inscriptions that are now illegible.

Penetrating into the interior, I stood at the threshold of a spacious vestibule, the entire length of which, measuring about a hundred and sixty feet, is covered with arabesques and sculptured figures of animals and men. On either side of the entrance stood three elephants of colossal size, with their drivers upon their necks and their houdahs upon their backs, in which, with great boldness, the unknown artist had fashioned a multitude of persons. The arched vault is sustained by two rows of pillars, each of which is also surmounted by an elephant, bearing upon his back a man and woman, in the form of cariatides, who seem to bend beneath the enormous weight they bear.

The interior is imposing but dismal, and it is impossible to find one's way in the prevailing darkness.

This grand underground crypt is a celebrated place of resort for pilgrims, and crowds of Fakirs are often met with, who have come from all parts of India, to perform their devotions in the Cave of Evocations.

Others live permanently in the neighborhood of the temple, where they spend the whole of their time in corporeal mortifications and mental contemplation, sitting, day and night, in front of two blazing fires, which are constantly fed by the attendants, who wear a band upon their mouth to prevent inhaling the slightest impurity, and eat nothing but a few grains of cooked rice, which they moisten with water filtered through a piece of linen cloth. They gradually arrive at a state of emaciation bordering closely upon death. Their moral strength is soon impaired, and when this protracted suicide has brought them to death's door, they have long been in such a state of intellectual and physical decrepitude that they hardly seem to be alive.

All Fakirs who strive to attain the highest transformations in the superior spheres have to undergo these terrible mortifications.

One was pointed out to me who had arrived some months ago from Cape Comorin, and who, sitting between two fires, in order, no doubt, to hasten the decomposition of his physical organs, had already arrived at a state of almost complete insensibility. Imagine my astonishment when, from a deep scar running across the whole upper part of his skull, I thought I recognized the Fakir of Trivanderam.

Approaching and addressing him in that beautiful Southern language in which he so much liked to converse, I asked him if he remembered the Franguy of Benares.

His almost lifeless eyes seemed to blaze up for a moment, and I heard him murmur the two Sanscrit words, which I had seen in phosphorescent letters on the evening of our last sitting:

Divyavapour gatwâ,

meaning, "I have clothed myself with a fluidic (fluidique) body."

That was the only sign of recognition that I was able to obtain. He was known to the Hindus in the neighborhood as Karli Sava, or the Karli Phantom.

So, decrepitude and imbecility appear to be the final end of all Hindu transformed Fakirs.

CONCLUSION.

In conclusion, we can only repeat the words of our preface:

"It is not our office to decide, either for or against, the belief in spirits, whether *mediating or inspiring.*"

Our aim is merely to give an account of the philosophical and spiritualistic tenets of the Brahmins, as well as of the external phenomena and manifestations which are, according to them, the means whereby the Pitris, or ancestral shades, demonstrate their existence and communicate with men.

All ancient religions, and even Christianity itself, acknowledge the existence of extraordinary beings, who have a special part to perform in the continuous movement of creation. All teach that man, upon laying aside his present earthly envelope, enters the superior world in the state of a spirit.

The constant perfectibility of the soul, and the spiritual life—that is their common philosophical idea.

As for the phenomena and manifestations, which are claimed to be supernatural, we also find them to be an outgrowth of this belief, both in the temples of India, Chaldea, and Egypt, and in the catacombs to which the early Christians fled for shelter.

We refrain from making any positive statement as to the possibility or not of the extraordinary phenomena performed by the Fakirs, as we have described them, which some attribute to the adroitest imposture and others to occult intervention, but leave the reader to judge for himself.